KEITH CHEETHAM was born in Sheffield in 1937. His boundless enthusiasm about the life of Mary Queen of Scots was sparked off in 1970 when, as a Member of Sheffield Junior Chamber of Commerce, he was given the task of organising a Mary, Queen of Scots Festival. In 1974 he was appointed as Sheffield's first Conference and Tourist Officer. In 1988 Keith set up a unit to market and develop England's Black Country as a tourist destination, a post he held until 1997 when he formed his own tourism consultancy, based in Wolverhampton.

His creative initiatives in the tourist field have gained him wide recognition. One of his most controversial was in 1982 when he promoted Mary Queen of Scots by organising a procession along Edinburgh's Royal Mile from the Castle to the Palace of Holyroodhouse. Mary was played by a tourist guide from Sheffield accompanied by Keith in the role of her longest-serving custodian, the 6th Earl of Shrewsbury. This event attracted wide publicity and Keith was dubbed by the media 'the man who sold Mary Queen of Scots to the Scots'.

A playwright and regular broadcaster on BBC Radio, he is author of the book *Mary Queen of Scots – The Captive Years*. He is chairman of an English branch of the Marie Stuart Society and has helped many tourist centres with information on Mary Queen of Scots. With his wide knowledge of Mary and the many sites associated with her in England, Scotland and France, he tells her story in uncomplicated style and clarifies many of the myths that have grown up around her.

D1410000

On the Trail of
Mary Queen of Scots

J. KEITH CHEETHAM

Luath Press Limited

EDINBURGH

www.luath.co.uk

This book is dedicated to my late parents,
Ruth and John Cheetham, who made everything possible for me.

First Edition 1999
Reprinted 2000

The paper used in this book is acid-free, neutral-sized and recyclable.
It is made from low chlorine pulps produced in a low energy,
low emission manner from sustainable forests.

Printed and bound by
Bell & Bain Ltd., Glasgow

Typeset in 10.5 point Sabon by
Senga Fairgrieve, Edinburgh, 0131 658 1763

Ride on, ride on in majesty!
In lowly pomp ride on to die;
Bow Thy meek head to mortal pain,
Then take, O God, Thy power, and reign.

Henry Hart Milman, 1791-1868

Acknowledgements

During the research, writing and compilation of this book, I have received an enormous amount of help, guidance and assistance from many people and organisations. I would like to single out, in particular, just a few who have given much of their time to help and, without whose wise counselling, factual information or checking of the manuscript, I could never have completed the job.

I owe a special debt of appreciation to the following friends in the Marie Stuart Society – Lilian Cameron, Lola and Norman Cash, Audrey Cartwright, Joy Childs, Margaret Lumsdaine, Myra McLanaghan, Ronald Morrison, Julie Pollard, and both Pauline and Syd Whitehead.

For additional information on France, I should like to thank Peter Wigley, who first opened the doors for my career in the tourist industry, and John Morgan. For information on Dragsholm Castle in Denmark, I am indebted to Annette V. Petersen and Niels Christian Ewald; and to Adrian Durkin on Dudley Castle. Others who have helped include Jill Fulton, Judith Sleigh, Anne I. Taylor, Roger Gilbride, John Pearson and Douglas Taylor.

The following bodies have also given me every co-operation – Churches Conservation Trust; Coventry, Oundle and Stamford Tourist Information Centres; Historic Scotland; Scottish Tourist Board; Clergy and Staff of Peterborough Cathedral; Sheffield City Libraries – Local Studies Section; Staffordshire Record Office; and Wolverhampton Reference Library.

I am also indebted to earlier authors on the subject, in particular Lady Antonia Fraser, the Duke of Hamilton and Professor Gordon Donaldson who have given me inspiration through their own authorative works.

Finally, I should like to single out my colleague, David Middleton, for his line drawings; Jim Lewis, cartographer; Catriona Scott, editor; Tom Bee of RedLetter; and my publishers at Luath Press Limited, Audrey and Gavin MacDougall, who have given me unstinting support and encouragement.

Contents

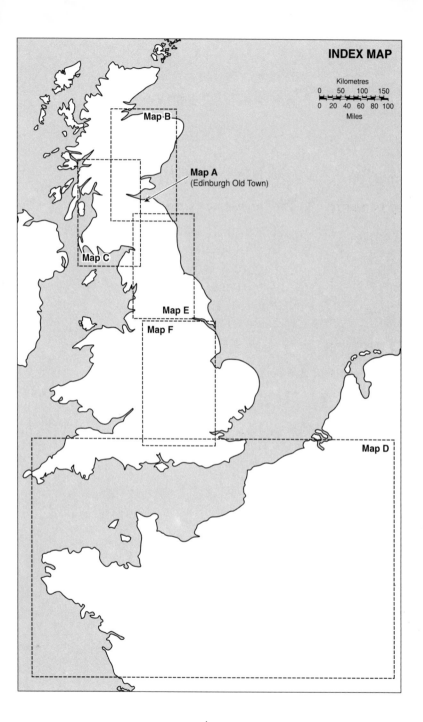

INDEX MAP

Kilometres
0   50   100   150
0 20 40 60 80 100
Miles

Map B

Map A
(Edinburgh Old Town)

Map C

Map E

Map F

Map D

Abbreviations

CCT	The Churches Conservation Trust
EH	English Heritage
HS	Historic Scotland
LT	The Landmark Trust
NTS	National Trust for Scotland
NT	National Trust – England

Addresses for the above organisations can be found on pages 174 and 175.

The page number given for each site on the maps which follow is the first page on which reference is made to the site.

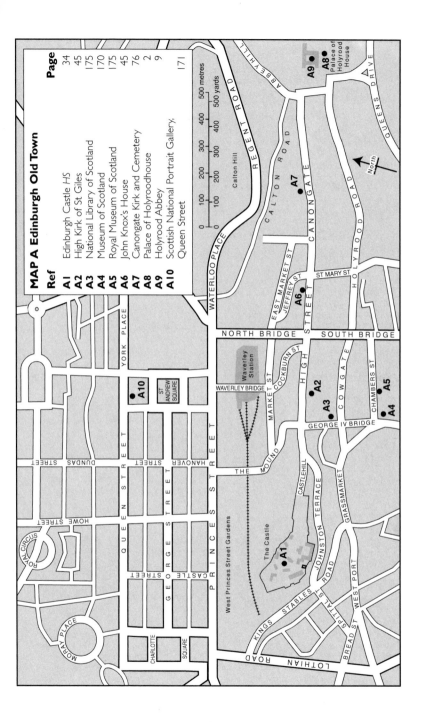

MAP A Edinburgh Old Town

xi

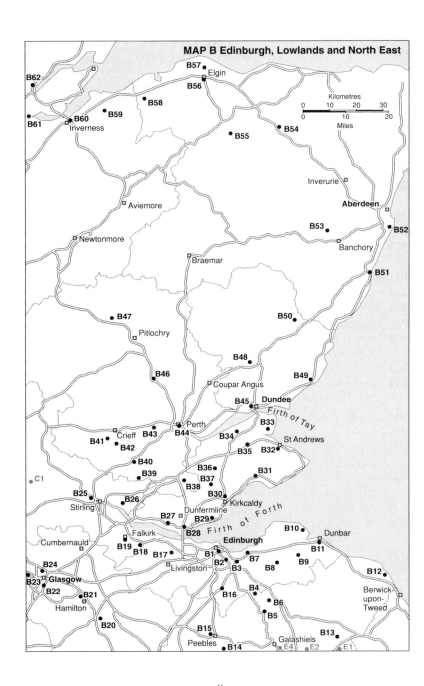

MAP B Edinburgh, Lowlands and North East

Kilometres
0 10 20 30
Miles
0   10   20

B62
B61
B60 Inverness
B59
B58
B57 • Elgin
B56
B55
B54
Inverurie
Aberdeen
B53
Banchory
B52
B51
Aviemore
Newtonmore
Braemar
B50
B47
Pitlochry
B48
B46
B49
Coupar Angus
B45 Dundee
Firth of Tay
Crieff
B41 B43
B42
B44 Perth
B34
B33
St Andrews
B35
B32
B40
B39
B36
B37
B31
C1
B38
B25 B26
B30
Stirling
Kirkcaldy
Dunfermline
B27
B29
Falkirk
B28 Firth of Forth
Cumbernauld
B19
B18
B17
B10
Dunbar
Edinburgh
B11
B24
B1
B7
B9
Livingston
B2
B3
B8
B12
Glasgow
B23
B22
B16
B4
Berwick-
upon-
Tweed
B21
B6
Hamilton
B5
B20
B13
B15
Galashiels
Peebles
B14
E4 E2 E1

xii

Edinburgh, Lowlands and North East

Key to Map B

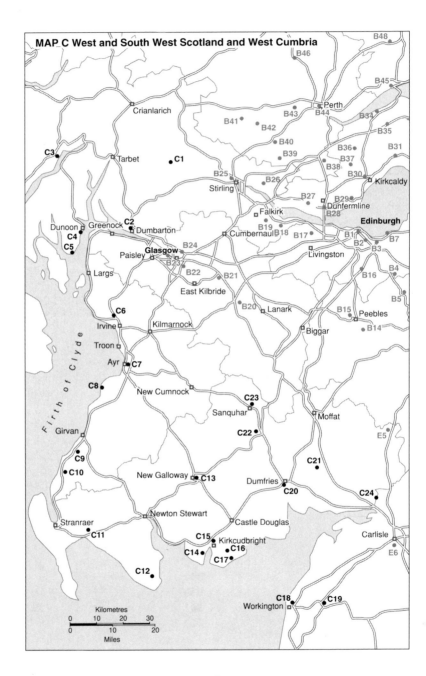

MAP C West and South West Scotland and West Cumbria

West and South West Scotland and West Cumbria

Key to Map C

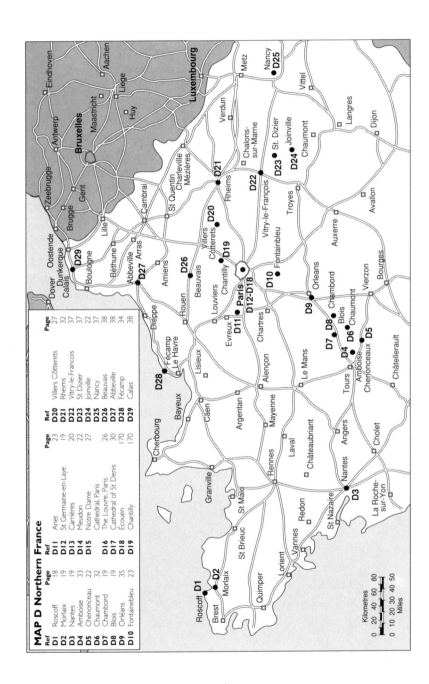

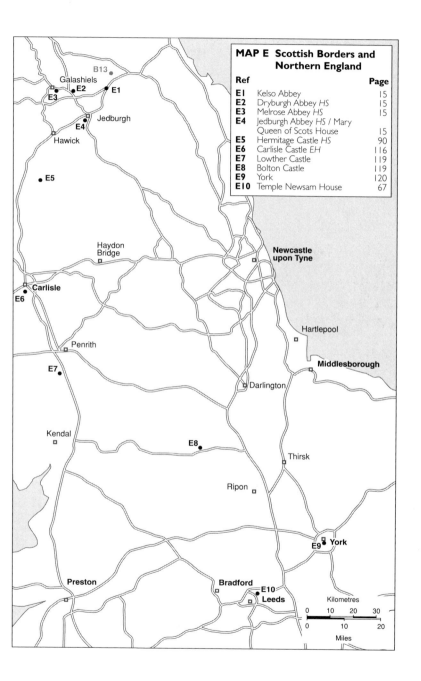

MAP E Scottish Borders and Northern England

Ref		Page
E1	Kelso Abbey	15
E2	Dryburgh Abbey *HS*	15
E3	Melrose Abbey *HS*	15
E4	Jedburgh Abbey *HS* / Mary Queen of Scots House	15
E5	Hermitage Castle *HS*	90
E6	Carlisle Castle *EH*	116
E7	Lowther Castle	119
E8	Bolton Castle	119
E9	York	120
E10	Temple Newsam House	67

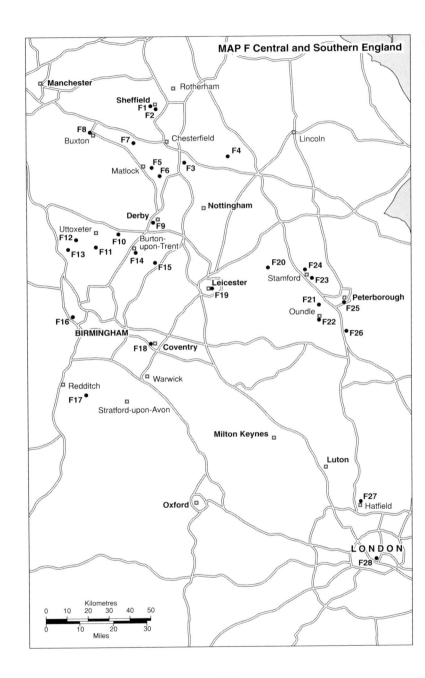

MAP F Central and Southern England

Manchester

Rotherham

Sheffield
F1
F2

F8
Buxton
F7
Chesterfield
Lincoln

F4

F5
Matlock
F6
F3

Nottingham

Derby
F9

Uttoxeter
F12
F10
Burton-
upon-Trent
F13
F11
F14
F15

F20
F24
Stamford
F23

Leicester
F19

F21
Peterborough
Oundle
F25
F16
F22
BIRMINGHAM
F26

F18
Coventry

Warwick

Redditch
F17
Stratford-upon-Avon

Milton Keynes

Luton

F27
Oxford
Hatfield

LONDON
F28

Kilometres
0   10   20   30   40   50

0   10   20   30
Miles

Central and Southern England

Key to Map F

Foreword

AS A BOY IN SHEFFIELD, I was often taken by my parents to visit my aunt and uncle who lived in Sutherland Road. This was situated in a steep valley in what was then a heavily-industrialised area of the east end of the city. Across the valley of the River Don, on the hillside opposite, stands a building which my father would always point out to me, saying, 'That is Sheffield Manor where Mary Queen of Scots was kept a prisoner!'

The first time I heard that statement, my interest was stirred. Why should a Queen of Scotland be held prisoner in Sheffield? At that point, I had only vaguely heard her name in history lessons at Firs Hill Junior School which I attended. I asked further questions and, to satisfy my curiosity, my father produced a book on local history, *The Story of Sheffield* by John Derry, published in 1915. It contained a chapter entitled 'Sheffield's Historical Prisoner' which gave a brief account of the Queen of Scots' life leading up to her nineteen years of imprisonment in England. The publication was illustrated with drawings of the various sites where the royal prisoner was held.

Over the years, my eagerness to discover more about this famous historical character grew, and it continued in manhood when, as a member of the local Junior Chamber of Commerce, I was invited to organise a major civic event. This was to commemorate the 400th anniversary of the arrival in Sheffield of the captive Queen of Scots on 28 November 1570. I got together a number of colleagues and, in the space of ten weeks, we arranged a Mary Queen of Scots festival.

I got more and more absorbed in research on Mary and it became an obsession. Looking back, I can confidently claim that my love affair with Mary Queen of Scots has lasted most of my life. As her story has unfolded, I have followed her movements and, in the process, fallen in love with Scotland and its people.

Mary's tale is a tragic one. It has all the ingredients which encompass the very essence of an historical thriller – ambition, greed, power, violence, sex, lust, murder, love and hatred. Throw in a beautiful queen surrounded by dashing beaux, blood-thirsty criminals and treacherous women, and the cocktail is complete.

The Queen of Scots, from her birth at Linlithgow Palace on 8 December 1542 to the time she met her death by the executioner's axe at Fotheringhay Castle on 8 February 1587, has fascinated millions of people down the years. What is so irresistibly magnetic about her that has attracted so much interest? Apart from her dynastic destiny and the turbulent events of her lifetime, her death left many questions unanswered. Most portraits of Mary give her an ethereal or angelic appearance but they do not really reflect the truth. Nobody who reads the story of Mary Queen of Scots can fail to be astonished by some of the foolish, miscalculated and bloody events which surrounded and involved her.

Mary's life was one long roller coaster. She moved through a series of disasters from Scotland to France, back to Scotland again, and finally to England, where she spent so many long years of imprisonment at the hands of her royal cousin, Elizabeth, the English Queen.

This book neither condones nor condemns, and I invite the reader to join me on a journey where we set out to trace the events of Mary's life and, along the way, visit many of the important sites associated with one of the most beautiful, enigmatic, yet tragic of queens ever to be recorded in Britain's history books.

J Keith Cheetham
May 1999

Introduction

SO MANY QUESTIONS WERE left unanswered after the death of Mary Queen of Scots. Should she have stayed in France after her first husband, Francis II, had died? Was she aware of the plot to murder her second husband, Lord Darnley? Did the Queen of Scots write the incriminating Casket Letters or were they forgeries? How could she, a Roman Catholic, have willingly agreed to take the divorced Earl of Bothwell as her third husband? And how deep was her involvement in the Babington Plot to murder Queen Elizabeth and seize the English throne with the help of her Catholic supporters?

Mary Stuart became Queen of Scots when she was only six days old and Queen Consort of France in her early teens. She also had a strong claim on the English throne which was occupied by Queen Elizabeth. One wonders what might have happened had England been ruled by Mary Stuart? Undoubtedly, the country would have reverted to Roman Catholicism as it had done earlier during the reign of Mary Tudor, half-sister to Elizabeth. For the story of Mary Queen of Scots is not only about a power struggle between two Queens – Elizabeth and Mary Stuart – it also had deep religious implications for the opposing Protestant and Roman Catholic faiths. In turn, these had repercussions on the Continent, and after Mary's death this led to the attempted invasion of England by the Spaniards in August 1588.

On fleeing from Scotland in 1568, would Mary have been better returning to France instead of throwing herself on Elizabeth's mercy? It was only to prove an escape into further captivity. Mary's standing in France had become of no real consequence when, as Dowager Queen after the death of her first husband, King Francis II, she departed for Scotland in 1561. She was hated at the French court by her mother-in-law, Catherine de Medici, who seized power through her younger son, Charles IX, when he inherited the throne on his elder brother's death. Perhaps Mary Queen of Scots could have gone into semi-retirement under the protection of her mother's relatives, the powerful Guise family, or confined herself in a convent of some religious order in France. If she had done the latter, she would undoubtedly have been able to live out her life in exile.

Had discretion and common sense been two of her attributes, she might have survived. Unfortunately, they were not, and she was carried along by the tide of life, forever clutching at straws in a fight for survival.

It is perhaps ironic that, despite her unsuccessful bid to claim the English throne, it was her son, James VI of Scotland, who eventually united the two kingdoms of Scotland and England when he succeeded Elizabeth in 1603 as King James I of England.

As we chart her progress and follow her trail from her birth at Linlithgow in 1542 to her death at Fotheringhay in 1587, it is in places such as the Palace of Holyroodhouse, Edinburgh Castle, Stirling Castle, and Bolton Castle in Yorkshire's Wensleydale that we best get a lingering sense of the days when the Queen of Scots passed through their corridors. But there are many more sites, occupied and unoccupied, intact and ruined where we may follow in her fascinating footsteps.

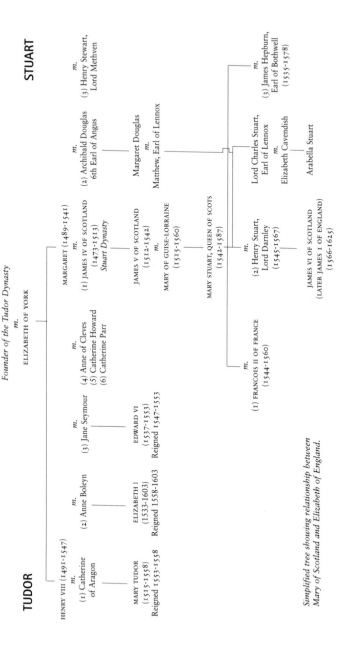

Simplified tree showing relationship between
Mary of Scotland and Elizabeth of England.

CHAPTER I

Fateful Dynasty

'THE FAULT, DEAR BRUTUS, is not in our stars but in ourselves.' So wrote William Shakespeare in Act One, Scene Two, of his play *Julius Caesar*. If England's Bard had written such dialogue for the fated Mary Queen of Scots, how appropriate it would have been. Her life story is a gift to any dramatist and I am sure that Shakespeare would have made a wonderful job of such a play. It was only much later that other playwrights, such as Friedrich Schiller (1759-1805), were to bring to life the tragic story of the Queen of Scots. Some have also taken delight in writing scenes in which the two Queens – Mary Stuart and Elizabeth – come face to face, creating for them a torrent of powerful words to fire at one another.

Despite various claims to the contrary, we can be fairly certain that they never actually met. Although Mary desired such an encounter, Elizabeth would never agree. And so all contact between them was done either through letters or by ministers, emissaries, envoys and other representatives of their courts. The English Queen was as cunning as a fox and every move she made concerning the Queen of Scots was played like a game of chess, everything carefully plotted before being executed.

In those far-off Tudor days, execution was almost a daily occurance. Few people in power could sleep safely in their beds at night without fear of betrayal or implication in some plot or other. Rivalry at court was rife as each new favourite jockeyed for position amongst his competitors.

In order to determine the root of the rivalry and hatred which existed between the two monarchs, we need to go back at least three generations to examine the dynastic links between the Royal Houses of England and Scotland – the Tudors and the Stewarts.

For centuries, the Scots and English had waged war on one another. At the beginning of the 16th century, the respective rulers – Henry VII of England and James IV of Scotland – wished their countries to live peaceably together. In order to bring about a closer relationship between the two nations, James married Margaret Tudor, elder daughter of the English King, in 1503. Under James's rule, there was stability and prosperity in Scotland and he encouraged business with many overseas countries. Edinburgh was declared the capital city and the Scottish Parliament began to meet there. The Palace of Holyroodhouse (A8) became home to the royal family.

Henry VII's successor in England was his second son, also named Henry, after the death of his elder son, Arthur, in 1502 at the age of fifteen. Arthur had just married Catherine of Aragon and, on his death, the young Henry not only became heir to the throne but also inherited his brother's wife in a second marriage treaty made between England and Spain. The new king showed himself to be ruthless, ambitious, greedy and anxious for power at whatever the cost to other people or countries. In 1513, he went to war with France, a country with which Scotland had long been allied through strong dynastic and political ties whereby the two countries would come to each other's aid in the event of war against England. Henry's action angered James IV and, in support of France, he invaded England. In September, he met the English at Flodden Field where a battle took place and the Scots were defeated. Sadly,

James was killed during the battle and was deeply mourned by his people.

His son, James V, was a mere infant of eighteen months when he inherited the throne of Scotland, which meant that a Regent had to be appointed. Some Scottish nobles preferred James's mother, the Dowager Queen Margaret Tudor; others were behind the Duke of Albany. There was much internal wrangling between the two sides and the infant King became a pawn in a game of politics and power. In 1528, when he felt he was old enough and equal to the task, he decided to rule Scotland alone.

As James V grew to manhood, the close alliance with the French was continued when he chose Princess Madeleine, daughter of King Francis I, as his bride. It was, however, well-known that he had already fathered a number of illegitimate children, of whom Lord James Stewart, the eldest, would play an important role in the life of Mary Queen of Scots.

After only a few months of marriage Madeleine died. James once again looked to France for a wife and he chose Mary of Guise, a member of one of France's most powerful families. She was the widow of the Duke of Longueville by whom she had had a son, Francis. She left him behind in France with his grandmother, Antoinette of Bourbon, wife of Claude, 1st Duke of Guise.

This marriage angered Henry VIII as he had also had designs on the fair lady. Catherine of Aragon, mother of Mary Tudor, had failed to give Henry a male heir and he grew tired of her. He courted and won the favours of Anne Boleyn, a member of his Court. Henry instructed his Lord Chancellor, Cardinal Wolsey, to begin negotiations with the Pope in Rome for a divorce on the grounds that he should never have been allowed to marry Catherine in the first place as she was his brother's widow. The Pope refused the request. Wolsey had to shoulder the blame and was stripped of all his offices. He was arrested on a trumped-up charge but, fortunately for him, he died at Leicester Abbey on his way to London to stand trial for high treason for he would undoubtedly have ended his days on the executioner's block.

Henry VIII appointed Sir Thomas More to succeed Wolsey, but he refused to condone a marriage to Anne Boleyn and paid with his life. (The play and films of *A Man For All Seasons* by Robert Bolt vividly depict this period of history.) Eventually, Thomas Cranmer was appointed as Archbishop of Canterbury and Henry instructed him to have the case heard in an English Church court rather than referring the matter to Rome. Cranmer grudgingly pronounced that the marriage was at an end and arrangements were immediately put in hand for Henry's wedding to Anne Boleyn in 1533. As expected, the marriage was declared illegal by the Roman Catholic Church – in their eyes, it was bigamous.

Henry responded by ordering his subjects to disobey the Pope's orders, renouncing the supremacy of His Holiness and breaking off all communications with Rome. By an Act of Supremacy, Henry proclaimed himself Head of the Church of England, and anyone who did not acknowledge him as such would be guilty of high treason.

He forced the clergy of both the English and Welsh Churches to excommunicate themselves from the papal authorities and ordered an immediate survey of all monasteries. He systematically closed all the church properties and sold them off to local families. This was done under the guise of suppressing corruption in the Church, but it was, in fact, a means for the king to acquire additional land and wealth for his own use.

Anne Boleyn was already pregnant when she married Henry and she bore the long-awaited child who would justify all his actions. To his extreme disappointment, the baby was a girl and was baptised Elizabeth. In the eyes of the Roman Catholic Church, the child was illegitimate, and this was to haunt Elizabeth to the end of her days. On 27 January 1536, Anne Boleyn miscarried a baby boy, the same day that Catherine of Aragon, his first wife, was buried in Peterborough Cathedral. Anne Boleyn's future as the English Queen Consort was short-lived. After learning of her alleged adultery, Henry began to seek a new wife whilst making arrangements to dispose of her.

On the day following Anne Boleyn's execution, Henry married Jane Seymour, daughter of a Wiltshire knight. Seventeen months later, in October 1537, she produced a son who was baptized Edward. At last, Henry had a legitimate male heir, as the marriage to Jane Seymour had taken place after the death of Catherine of Aragon, his legitimate wife as defined by the Roman Catholic Church. The baby was born by Caesarean section and Jane Seymour died.

Henry chose his next wife, Anne of Cleves, for diplomatic reasons and on the strength of a portrait painted by Hans Holbein. The image was very different from the person who arrived from Germany to marry Henry and he found her appearance repulsive. Henry nicknamed her 'The Flanders Mare' and six months later, after non-consummation of the marriage, they were divorced. Anne of Cleves managed to stay on reasonable terms with the king which perhaps saved her from an early and unpleasant death.

In the same year, 1540, Henry married Catherine Howard, a cousin of Anne Boleyn and niece of the Duke of Norfolk. It was not long before her extra-marital activities came to Henry's ears and, within eighteen months of her marriage, she was charged with misconduct and ended her life on the block. Finally, Henry married his sixth wife, Catherine Parr, a discreet and caring young widow who faithfully nursed the ageing monarch throughout his later years.

Henry died on 28 January 1547 and was succeeded by his only son, Edward, who was nine years old. A delicate infant, his poor health meant he never lived long enough to reign without a Council of Regency. By 1553, it became obvious he had little time left to live. The next in line to the throne was his elder half-sister, Princess Mary, daughter of Henry VIII and Catherine of Aragon. She was a devout Catholic and unlikely to maintain the Protestant faith as the Established Church of England. To avoid this happening, Edward was persuaded to make a will leaving the crown to his cousin, Lady Jane Grey, a great-granddaughter of Henry VII. The young King died in July 1553.

Lady Jane Grey was a girl of only seventeen when she inherited the throne and was married to Lord Guildford Dudley. As soon as she was proclaimed Queen, a warrant was issued for the arrest of the rightful heir, Princess Mary Tudor. Mary managed to escape to Suffolk where the people rallied to her support and paid homage to her as their Queen. Pursued by a Protestant army led by the Duke of Northumberland, she went to London where the citizens came out in support of her. The army, in turn, deserted Northumberland, who was tried for high treason and executed. Mary was then proclaimed Queen Mary I. Lady Jane Grey and her husband were committed to the Tower of London and executed. Bloody times indeed!

The coming to the throne of Queen Mary Tudor brought about a resurgence of the Roman Catholic faith in England. She married Philip II of Spain, son and heir of the Emperor Charles V, the most powerful monarch in Europe. However, Mary was unable to produce an heir and on her death in 1558 Elizabeth succeeded her as Queen of England and Protestantism regained control as the Established Church. However, a shadow had fallen across the English throne – a threat from the House of Stewart in Scotland.

The marriage between James V and Mary of Guise had been fruitful and produced a healthy baby girl, Mary, on 8 December 1542 at the Palace of Linlithgow. Alas, her father only lived a few more days and the infant Mary was proclaimed Queen of Scots when she was six days old. Mary was a granddaughter of Margaret Tudor, elder sister of Henry VIII, whose House, after the death of Queen Mary Tudor, should have been next in line to the throne of England, according to the Roman Catholic Church. The young Mary Queen of Scots, was, in its opinion, the rightful heir to the throne of England – not Elizabeth. The argument about

Elizabeth's alleged illegitimacy was to rage on for years and led to a fight to the bitter end between the two Queens for there could only be one outcome – one would eventually destroy the other.

Shortly before her death in February 1587, Mary Queen of Scots embroidered a cloth of estate with these words, 'In my end is my beginning'. Ominous words indeed.

CHAPTER 2

Early Years

DURING EARLY NOVEMBER 1542, Mary of Guise was at Linlithgow awaiting the birth of her third child, having already lost two sons in infancy. The traditional place of confinement for members of the Scottish royal family was the Palace of Linlithgow (B18). We start our journey at this fortress, set beside a quiet loch, midway between the two strongholds of Edinburgh and Stirling. The Palace and adjacent Kirk of St Michael stand in an elevated position on a promontory on the southern shore of Linlithgow Loch.

A manor house of wood and a church of stone were first erected on the site in the 12th century. In 1301-2, Edward I of England enclosed the buildings with a palisade of wooden towers. After the Scottish War of Independence the manor house was rebuilt by King David II. It was destroyed by fire in 1424. The Palace of Linlithgow was commenced the following year by James I of Scotland. During the reign of his grandson, James III, repair work was carried out. James IV did much to enhance the buildings by

Linlithgow Palace

adding stairs, galleries and new passages. Particularly eye-catching is the ornate fountain with its exquisite carvings which is sited in the centre of the quadrangle. James IV's wife, Margaret Tudor, was in residence at Linlithgow when she was brought news of the death of her husband at Flodden. James V, born at the Palace in 1515, was responsible for developing the site to its complete quadrangular shape and he transferred the main entrance from the east to the south side. When he brought his new Queen, Mary of Guise, to Linlithgow for the first time, it is reported that she took great delight in what she found and declared it 'the most princely home she had looked upon'.

While Mary of Guise was awaiting the birth, James V was absent with his army which was fighting at Solway Moss (C24), close to the English border near the River Esk. The King had been taken ill and was actually at Caerlaverock Castle when the battle took place. The English troops routed the Scots and many soldiers were slain. James was wounded and taken to Edinburgh, then on to Hallyards near Dunfermline in Fife. He managed to spend a few days with his Queen at Linlithgow in the later stage of her pregnancy. The weakening King was moved to Falkland Palace (B36), one of his favourite hunting residences, where he spent his final days. He was defeated, broken-hearted and near to death when a messenger brought tidings from Linlithgow. His Queen had been safely delivered of a baby daughter on 8 December 1542. When he heard the news and told it was a girl, James reputedly made the remark, 'It cam wi' a lass, and will gang wi' a lass', by which he meant that the House of Stewart's royal line began with the daughter of Robert the Bruce marrying a Stewart, and it would also end with a woman. This did not, in fact, happen until the early 18th century, when Queen Anne, the last in line of the Stewart monarchs, died.

Six days later, James V died at Falkland Palace and was taken to Holyrood Abbey (A9) in Edinburgh for burial. Falkland Palace, in a picturesque Royal burgh of quaint streets and old houses, was built on the site of a castle, the home of the MacDuff family. The castle came into possession of James II and became a royal residence. It was the principal hunting lodge of Scottish monarchs from the 12th century. James IV completed the main structure of the Palace with the addition of the east and south ranges. It was a favourite seat of the Scottish court from the time of James V who did much to improve its amenities and had it re-designed in French Renaissance style. The royal tennis courts, built by James V in 1539, and the 'lang butts', where members of the royal family were accustomed to practice archery, still exist. The building gives a real sense of history, and in the quiet of a summer evening, Falkland is a peaceful place to wander around, especially when the setting sun sinks behind the nearby rolling Lomond Hills.

The infant Queen was christened in the Kirk of St Michael, adjacent to Linlithgow Palace, a few days after her father's death. This church was first consecrated in 1242 by the Bishop of St Andrews. A fire at the Palace in 1424 severely damaged the church and re-building was commenced and completed a century later. Over the years it has been closely associated with many great figures in Scottish history including James IV, Mary Queen of Scots, and, later, Prince Charles Edward Stuart.

Mary was born in a room in the north-west tower of Linlithgow Palace and for the next nine months was nursed there. However, the immediate problem of a young child acceding to the throne was that of government and who would act as Regent until the monarch reached maturity. Another matter was also looming on the horizon – King Henry VIII, the English King, knew that the birth of the little Queen of Scots at the same time as the death of James V, might work in his favour. For years, France and Scotland had been enemies of England, and more French influence had been introduced into the Scottish court with the arrival of Mary of Guise. In Henry's eyes, the situation was threatening, if a joint initiative were to be mounted by those two countries against his own. He had long coveted Scotland, and some form of alliance through the new infant in Scotland could be a major stepping stone to his ambition to make it part of his kingdom. In any case, he already claimed to be overlord of that country after having defeated the Scottish army.

Henry's marriage to Jane Seymour had produced a son and heir for the English throne, Edward, who was five years old. A union of marriage between the newly-born Queen of Scots and his son would be a means of achieving his goal. At the Battle of Solway Moss on 24 November 1542, the English had taken many Scottish nobles as prisoners. They had been escorted to London and Henry was to use them as bargaining tools in his lust for power – they would be given their freedom and a pension if, on their return to Scotland, the infant Mary was delivered into his guardianship.

On the question of a Scottish Regent, the person who had the most credible hereditary claim was James, Earl of Arran, who was later to become the 1st Duke of Châtelherault. His pedigree was good, since his grandfather, the first Lord Hamilton, had been married to Mary Stewart, the sister of James III, which meant he was next in line to the throne. (The only shadow of doubt was whether his father had been properly divorced from his second wife, and as he was the child of the third marriage, there was a question of illegitimacy surrounding him.) However, he was not considered suitable. For a start, he was a staunch supporter of the new Protestant faction that was advancing in Scotland, in particular amongst some of the nobility.

Alternatives for the Scottish Regency included members of the Lennox-Stewart family who were descended from the same Mary Stewart and Lord Hamilton through the female line. This meant that they also considered they had a strong claim as heirs to the throne – and their claim was legitimate. So the Earl of Lennox rather than the Earl of Arran had the stronger case to become Regent.

The Earl of Lennox had gone to France in 1532 at the age of

sixteen and was educated there. On the death of James v, he was induced by Cardinal Beaton of St Andrews to return to Scotland. Lennox allied himself to England and offered himself as bridegroom to the Lady Margaret Douglas, daughter of Margaret Tudor, elder sister to Henry viii. They were the parents of Henry Stuart, Lord Darnley, who was later to play a major role in Mary's story.

Arran had an enemy in the Cardinal Archbishop of St Andrews, who opposed his Protestant leanings. Beaton was immoral and cruel, but was highly experienced in the affairs of European politics. He was a supporter of the Roman Catholics in France in their opposition to the attitude and actions of Henry viii of England against the Church of Rome. The Cardinal Archbishop considered himself to be of far greater intelligence than Arran and he was also one of the greatest opponents of the Protestant faith. It was natural that Mary of Guise would side with her own Church of Rome over the question of the Regency and she therefore gave her support to Beaton. In turn, their opponents used the opportunity to start spreading tales of an affair between the two, but there was no actual proof.

Irrespective of the Cardinal Archbishop's actions, the governing factor was the return of the Scottish noblemen who had been taken prisoner at Solway Moss. Whilst in England, they had been forced by Henry viii to sign documents that would promote a marriage alliance between his son, Edward, and the infant Mary Queen of Scots. Monetary contributions also came their way with their support for this. They threw their weight behind the Protestant Arran, and the result was that James, Earl of Arran, was appointed as Regent.

Arran was not without ambition and had been keen to see his own son married to the Queen of Scots. Henry heard of the plan and so he offered Arran his younger daughter, Elizabeth Tudor, who was then ten years old. With his own safety and well-being in mind, Arran wisely decided not to oppose Henry nor to accept his offer.

A Treaty of Greenwich was therefore drawn up on 1 July 1543 when documents were prepared and signed to confirm the marriage of Prince Edward of England to Mary Queen of Scots. Henry then demanded that the infant Mary be brought to England to be brought up and trained within his own court. Mary of Guise, who had left her first son behind in France and had lost two infant sons, was horrified at the thought that she might have her only daughter taken away from her, all the more so knowing that Henry was such a ruthless, brutal ruler and directly opposed to her own religious belief. Far better, if she had to part with her child, to send her to the court of France.

Arran was a ditherer who was unable to negotiate or make up his mind one way or the other. Cardinal Beaton was a much stronger character who would have stood up to Henry after his break with the Church of Rome. Henry had the audacity to try to persuade the Cardinal to abandon his links with Rome so that the two of them might become friends. It was to no avail. After more indecision, Arran was finally persuaded to give his support to the French alternative and he received the sacrament of the Roman Catholic church. This blatant defiance angered Henry and he decided that peaceable methods were no longer appropriate to achieve what he wanted. Direct military action would be taken. Thus began a period of history that has been described as the Rough Wooing.

By now the Scots nobles had lost all patience with the English King and moved the infant Mary from Linlithgow Palace to Stirling Castle (B25). She was crowned Queen of Scots in the Chapel Royal of the Castle on 9 September 1543 whilst seated on her mother's knee. The little Queen was only nine months old.

Stirling Castle is set in a dramatic position on a steep rocky escarpment. The first evidence of a wooden fortification there dates back to the 11th century. The castle stands high above the meandering River Forth, which provided an important trade route into the area, at a point in Central Scotland where Lowlands meet

Highlands. It was a strategic military position, particularly useful during the 13th and 14th century Wars of Independence. Two of the most famous battles in Scottish history were fought in the vicinity to regain control of the castle from English forces. These were the Battle of Stirling Bridge in 1297 and the Battle of Bannockburn in 1314.

The present royal buildings in Stirling Castle date from the reigns of James IV and James V. These include the palace, completed in 1542 and worked on by French stonemasons, a ploy by James V to make an impression on his wife, Mary of Guise. There are two squares in the main part of the castle, the upper one surrounded by royal apartments including the King's House and the Chapel Royal. Many of the buildings contain magnificent Renaissance architecture and much restoration work has been carried out over recent years. In particular, work on the Great Hall has been a multi-million pound operation lasting a good number of years. It is due to be completed at the beginning of the new Millennium.

The castle is reached by climbing up a steep hill through the 'auld toun'. Numerous historic buildings have been lovingly preserved, especially Argyll's Lodging, the finest and most complete surviving example in Scotland of a 17th-century town residence. It was the home of the Earl of Argyll around 1680. Nearby stands the Church of the Holy Rude where Mary's son, James VI, was crowned King on 29 July 1567. The Old Town Jail is also open to visitors. During summer months, local actors carry out a series of ghost walks around the Old Town graveyard and surrounding area.

Undoubtedly, the breakdown of the relationship between Arran and Cardinal Beaton and the English King helped strengthen the links between Scotland and France. Scotland was a poor country and France, through Mary of Guise, assisted the Scots by providing military force to help them resist the English advances. It was recognised that the ties between the two countries could be strengthened further by a marriage between Mary Queen of Scots and the heir to the throne of France, the Dauphin Francis.

Henry VIII, fully realising the outcome of the proposal, threw his full force against the Scots. He despatched the Earl of Hertford with an army to wage war on Scotland and take the young Queen Mary by force. He instructed his troops to inflict every misery they could, to plunder the country, capture Edinburgh and Leith (B1) and set fire to any place and kill anyone who tried to prevent them carrying out his violent plan. This resulted in the widespread destruction of many towns in Southern Scotland and the desecration of the great Border abbeys of Melrose (E3), Dryburgh (E2), Kelso (E1) and Jedburgh (E4), the English army laying waste the country on the march northwards.

A major battle took place at Pinkie Cleugh near Musselburgh on 10 September 1547 as the English forced their way further into Scotland, taking Edinburgh and Leith. They fought on in the direction of Stirling where the young Queen was living. English garrisons were also set up in South-East Scotland. The net was tightening around the little monarch, and Stirling Castle was considered unsafe for her. It was arranged that, along with her mother and four of her playmates, better known throughout history as the Queen's Four Maries, Mary would be taken clandestinely by night to Inchmahome Priory (C1) for greater safety.

Inchmahome Priory is set on a small island in the middle of the Lake of Menteith, in the area now known as The Trossachs. It is a 13th-century Augustinian priory laid out according to the arrangement of a religious house – a spacious kirk with conventional buildings grouped round a cloister on its southern side. There was a Chapter House, Cloister Walk, an Inner Parlour and a Warming House. The island and its buildings, with its trees, ancient walls, corridors and stairs, would have made an ideal place for the young children to play. It is said that whilst Mary was at Inchmahome, she began to learn a few words of Spanish, Italian and Latin under the watchful eyes of the monks. Her mother, Mary of Guise, would undoubtedly have spoken mostly in French to her young daughter, something Mary was soon to find useful.

The names of the little Queen's four friends all happened to be Mary and all came from the Scottish nobility. There was Mary Seton (who was to stay with the Queen of Scots for many years into later life), Mary Beaton, Mary Livingston and Mary Fleming. Each had been selected to serve the Queen through their family links with the Royal House of Stewart and with France. They were great comfort and company for Mary during her early years.

You can take a boat trip from the Port of Menteith to the island of Inchmahome to explore the ruins of the old priory. The island is an enchanting place, especially later in the year when autumn tints are at their most colourful. As well as the ruins of the ancient abbey, there is a modern monument to the great Scottish patriot and writer, R. B. Cunninghame Graham, who is buried there. The garden of the monastery is known as The Queen's Garden, whilst nearby is a Queen Mary's Tree and a Queen Mary's Bower, which all add a little romance to any visit.

In the following June, the French king's envoy, André de Montalembert, arrived. Mary of Guise knew that her daughter was in great danger of being kidnapped and abducted if she remained in Scotland and their hiding place was discovered. In her opinion, the only safe place for Mary would be the court of France. There she could be protected, schooled and brought up in a manner to fully embrace the Roman Catholic faith, learn court etiquette, foreign languages and subjects she would later need in her role as Queen. There was also the prospect of her proposed marriage to the Dauphin, Francis. In addition, she would be guarded and watched over by her own people, the powerful Guise family. The alternative was the risk of her capture by the English and being forcibly removed to the court of Henry VIII to an uncertain future and possible danger. Mary of Guise's mind was made up. Despite the bitter thought of having to part with her beloved daughter, she decided that Mary must be sent to France.

Arrangements were made for the young Queen, her mother, the four Maries and other young children of the Scottish court to make the journey to Dumbarton Castle (C2), a fortification situated on a volcanic rock on the northern bank of the River Clyde. The royal party had to wait there for the French king's boats to arrive to convey them to the safety of France and the comfort of the French court. The day of embarkation was set for 29 July, but it was not until 7 August that the weather was considered calm enough for the galleys to set sail. Mary was only five years old. The first chapter in her turbulent life was already over. Her return to Scotland would be under very different circumstances.

CHAPTER 3

France

THE JOURNEY TO FRANCE took Mary Stewart and her fellow passengers down the River Clyde, into the Irish Sea, then round Land's End to cross the English Channel. After six days, they arrived at the little port of Roscoff (D1) on the northern coast of Brittany on 13 August 1548. It is ironic that Prince Charles Edward Stuart was also to land at this point two hundred years later after his defeat at Culloden.

Mary had with her a good company of young friends including the four Maries, young relatives – three of her half-brothers, one of whom was James Stewart – and other supporters. In total, there were over one hundred lords and ladies plus her governess, Lady Fleming, and a nurse and four ships were needed to carry her retinue to France. She herself travelled in Henry II's royal galley. Despite the hazardous crossing of the Channel for the young Queen, the journey would be the beginning of a new adventure. In addition,

Chenonceau

there was the excitement of meeting many of her French relations in the Guise family for the first time.

Roscoff today is a popular fishing resort well-known for its lobsters. It has a Gothic cathedral church, Notre Dame de Croac Batz, completed in 1545, which has a remarkable Renaissance belfry with lantern turrets. At the edge of the beach is a granite house called La Maison de Marie Stuart – No 25 in the rue Amiral Revellière. There is a plaque on the wall which reads 'Sur le grève, à l'emplacement de la rampe d'accès, Marie Stuart débarqua en Août 1548'. ('This is the spot where Marie Stuart stepped ashore in August 1548.') There is a small tower near the seafront dedicated to the Queen of Scots at the point where the royal party first set foot on French soil.

Leaving Roscoff, they made for Morlaix (D2), where Mary spent the night in a convent founded by Saint Dominic. This picturesque town, which is dominated by a huge viaduct, is located at the confluence of two rivers which flow through a deep valley. There are many historic buildings, including the house of Anne of Brittany which was visited by Mary. Anne became Queen of France at the beginning of the 16th century when she married Louis XII.

Mary's route was then across country to the town of Nantes (D3) situated at the confluence of the Rivers Erdre and Loire. It was the capital of Brittany in the 15th century (after the French Revolution Nantes ceased to be part of Brittany and was made capital of the Loire-Atlantique Département), and prosperity came mainly from its maritime background. The novelist, Jules Verne, was born in Nantes in 1828 and there is a museum devoted to his life at 3 rue de l'Hermitage.

The next bit of the journey was by boat along the River Loire, passing the lovely châteaux of Blois (D8) and Chambord (D7) which were later to feature so prominently in Mary's life at the French court.

The eventual destination was the château of Saint Germain-en-Laye (D12) where the French royal family was officially in residence at the time. (The composer, Claude Debussy (1862-1918) was born at St Germain.) The town had grown up around a strategically sited fortress that commanded this reach of the River Seine. Built to the west of Paris, on a high escarpment overlooking a meandering stretch of the river, it is backed by the vast forest of Saint Germain. Work on the new château began in 1539 under the direction of the architect Pierre de Chambiges but, according to one authority, Francis I 'took such an interest that one could well say that he was the architect'. It was entirely rebuilt except for the keep and chapel. Later, it became the residence of Henrietta Maria of England and, after 1688, of the exiled English king, James II, (James VII of Scotland) who died there in 1701. It was during the same period that the town became a hotbed of Jacobite intrigue. In the church opposite the château is a tomb of James II where his heart is buried.

Before reaching Saint Germain, Mary was introduced to her grandmother, Duchess Antoinette of Guise, who accompanied her for the last stage of the journey. She was able to explain some of the etiquette expected of her granddaughter when she reached the French court. The Duchess was quite a formidable though good-humoured lady who lived to a ripe old age and outlived eleven of her twelve children. She had a good grasp of the affairs of state, a trait which had been inherited by her daughter, Mary of Guise.

Prior to Mary's arrival at Saint Germain, preparations were in hand to clean the château, and the French royal children were, in fact, at the nearby fortification of Carrières (D13) when the Queen of Scots and her entourage stopped off there. It was the start of a very happy and carefree period in her young life. This was her first meeting with her future husband, the Dauphin, Francis, and an early bond between the two was soon apparent.

The dazzle and sophistication of life at the court of France would have been in marked contrast to the rather dour lifestyle Mary would have been used to in Scotland. There was much music and dancing, and almost any excuse would be used for a celebration. From their time in the nursery and throughout their lives, royal children would have been protected, fawned over, cosseted, spoiled and indulged.

* * *

French influence in Scotland increased through Mary's alliance with the court of France. Arran, the Regent in her absence, was soon bought off by the French by being elevated to Duke of Châtelherault. In 1544, he was prevailed upon to resign as Regent in favour of Mary's mother Mary of Guise. John Knox, who was to be the bane of Mary's life, returned to Scotland from French imprisonment, and movements were afoot to replace the Roman Catholic faith in Scotland with Protestantism. Lord James Stewart, Mary's half-brother, was in command of the Reformers. Riots in many parts of Scotland forced Mary of Guise to introduce disciplinary measures in her daughter's absence. This did not augur well for the future.

* * *

Henry II of France had been married to his Queen, Catherine de Medici, for ten years before she had any children. For a long time it was thought Catherine was barren. She experimented with a number of so-called remedies or potions in an effort to conceive. Eventually she was successful, and her first child, Francis, arrived in 1544. He was a sickly boy from the day he was born. Nine other children followed in quick succession, including two who would also become King of France. Three died in infancy. As well as the maternal care they received from Catherine de Medici, the royal children were also influenced by another strong character – their father's mistress, Diane de Poitiers, who took an equal share in the upbringing of the children. Diane was twenty years older than King Henry and had a strong hold over the royal household. She more or less ran the court and relished her power. The King gave her a present of the beautiful château of Chenonceau (D5), much to the disapproval of Catherine.

Mary's Guise relatives consisted of six uncles and three aunts, some of whom were among the most powerful people in France. The most important of her uncles were Francis, the 2nd Duke of Guise, and Charles, who was the ambitious Cardinal of Lorraine. Both had much influence in state matters, especially during the time when their niece was Queen Consort. They were particularly anxious that the young Queen of Scots should be thoroughly indoctrinated into Roman Catholicism.

The favourite Guise family house was the château at the town of Joinville (D24) on the River Marne. The Château du Grand-Jardin stands in a park to the north of the town and was built by Mary's grandfather, Claude of Lorraine, 1st Duke of Guise, for his wife, Antoinette. It was badly damaged during the French Revolution of 1789, but two alabaster statues from the tomb of the 1st Duke of Guise can be seen in the local Hôtel de Ville.

Another Guise château was at Meudon (D14), south-west of central Paris. The stately Avenue du Château is lined with four rows of lime trees. Half-way down the avenue a plaque on the left marks the house where Richard Wagner composed the score of his opera, *The Flying Dutchman*. A manor house had stood on the site of the château of the House of Guise since the 15th century and became the property of the mistress of King Francis I who added two new wings and a park. It was later sold to Mary Stewart's uncle, the Cardinal of Lorraine. The château remained in Guise family ownership for a century, after which, due to financial difficulties, it had to be sold. In 1706, Louis XIV demolished part of the site and replaced it with a new building to include private apartments for his son. It fell into disrepair until in 1793, the chemist Berthollet and Général Choderlos de Laclos jointly set up a military research centre. In 1804 a fire damaged the building so badly that it had to be demolished. A new château was built at Meudon by Madame Pompadour, mistress of Louis XV, in the mid-18th century. Little remains of the original château apart from two small wings. Restoration of the central part took place at a later date and it now houses an observatory.

The Guise's main base in Paris was the Hôtel de Guise which was situated in the Marais district.

Mary soon began to settle in to life at the French court. In the nursery she improved on her few words of Latin – the language of the Roman Catholic church, and learnt Spanish and Italian, the latter the native tongue of Catherine de Medici. She had learned something of these languages from the monks at Inchmahome Priory in Scotland. Perhaps to encourage Mary to speak in French, the four Maries were sent away to a Dominican convent school for a period until they were older and were later allowed to rejoin their mistress.

Mary was also taught handwriting. As there was no 'W' in the French language, she began to spell her name Stuart instead of Stewart (it will be spelt Stuart from here on). Together with other royal children, she received a thorough schooling in the culture of France. She was also taught to ride and became an expert horsewoman. This was to prove a great asset to the Queen in later years, especially when she had to endure several hurried and sometimes undignified removals from one place to another.

According to Lady Antonia Fraser's authoritative account, *Mary Queen of Scots,* during the court year the children of the royal nursery were moved around between several palaces. These included Fontainebleau (D10), Anet (D11), the home of Diane de Poitiers close to St. Germain, Blois (D8) in the Loire Valley, and Chambord (D7), the largest of all the châteaux on the Loire.

Fontainebleau owes its origins to royalty's passion for hunting and collecting works of art. The forest of Fontainebleau was a favourite sporting ground for French monarchs but it was not until the reign of Francis I that the hunting lodge became a palace. The monarchy had a passion for collecting works of art and amassed them at Fontainebleu. Francis I commissioned a number of Florentine artists and sculptors to work on the château. After his death, Henry II continued building work and, in particular, created the magnificent ballroom. Fontainebleu is one of the most popular destinations for excursions from central Paris.

Anet (D11) was built by Henry II, between 1548 and 1555, as a gift for Diane. The architect was Philibert Delorme and the decoration is by Benvenuto Cellini, Pilon and Goujon. Only the entrance gate survives along with the beautiful domed chapel in which Mary Stuart and the other royal children used to worship with Diane de Poitiers. The entrance gate is decorated with a replica of Cellini's Nymph of Fontainebleau (the original is in the Louvre), above which is a clock surmounted by a sculptured stag hunt. Beyond the gate is all that remains of the château with a vestibule and staircase added by the Duc de Vendôme in the 17th century. There are panelled rooms containing portraits, tapestries and other memorabilia connected with Diane and the history of the once-great mansion. The tomb of Diane was desecrated at the Revolution but her remains were rescued and re-buried outside the east end of the local 13th-century parish church.

The château at Blois (D8) is in a commanding position on the northern bank of the Loire and overlooks the quaint streets and houses of the lower town. The building encloses a large courtyard. The sumptuous wing to the north built by Francis I contains rich, unusual furnishings, monumental fireplaces and wonderful staircases including one which was used for viewing hunts and jousts. The apartments of Catherine de Medici are on the first floor, and include the bedroom in which she died on 5 January 1589 and a study which was known as the Cabinet des Poisons. In this room there are secret panels behind which Catherine is thought to have hidden the potions which she used during her many efforts to conceive. There are 237 carved panels, four of which open by means of a secret device to reveal hidden cupboards.

A gallery leads to the Tour des Oubliettes and a cell where Henry, the 3rd Duke of Guise, Mary's cousin, was assassinated on 22 December 1588.

Chambord (D7) is situated on the wooded outskirts of the Sologne, south of the Loire. It is a prime example of French

Renaissance architecture and Leonardo de Vinci (1452-1519) was responsible for the design. Originally a hunting lodge used by the counts of Blois, work was begun by Francis I around 1519. It is said that 1,800 workmen were employed on the building over a period of fifteen years. The château with its white walls and cylindrical turrets of slate at each corner is entirely symmetrical and measures 156m in length by 117m wide. Chambord has 440 rooms, 315 fireplaces, 15 main staircases and 70 secondary ones, but its greatest glory is the double spiral staircase where people go up and down in sight of one another but without actually meeting.

The French dramatist, Molière, had close associations with Chambord. He wrote *Monsieur de Pourceaugnac* at the château and other plays of his were performed there.

The massive complex is surrounded by an enormous park where herds of wild boar, deer and sheep roam freely. Perhaps the best way to approach the château is to arrive along the drive. It is initially completely obscured from view by woodland, but gradually, as you get closer, the full grandeur of the situation opens up to reveal the exquisite building. However, a word of warning. You are likely to discover that the architectural glory of the exterior of many châteaux does, in the main, surpass the actual contents of their various rooms. Many treasures and family heirlooms were stolen or confiscated during the French Revolution and the interiors are often sparse. The desecration also caused much exterior damage, and for many of the buildings which are open to visitors today one must thank the skill and labour of modern-day sculptors and stonemasons who have restored much of the stonework and woodwork to their original design. Chambord is a typical example of this.

The châteaux of the Loire include some of the most famous historical monuments in France and they are carefully maintained by the State or private owners. Unfortunately, there are no organisations quite like The National Trusts for Scotland and England, Historic Scotland and English Heritage, and many smaller châteaux have been either neglected or sold off to the highest bidder, often to the detriment of the national heritage.

Two years after her arrival in France, Mary was overjoyed to receive a visit from her mother, Mary of Guise, and they spent several happy months in each other's company. The main purpose of the visit was to ask the French King for more military assistance for Scotland in an effort to quell the growing movement towards Protestantism within the Reformation. When the time came for Mary of Guise to depart for Scotland, it was upsetting for the young Queen and another disappointment was that her governess, Lady Fleming, was also to return home. The reason for this was that she had disgraced herself by having an affair with the French king and becoming pregnant by him.

The Queen of Scots, having grown into a tall and beautiful young woman, was a favourite of King Henry. Over the years, Mary and her future husband, Francis, had become close. Although, unofficially, the young couple had been betrothed as infants, thoughts began to turn towards cementing the union as they moved toward maturity. In the autumn of 1557, the King invited nine Scottish commissioners, including Mary's half-brother, Lord James Stewart, to discuss and confirm a marriage contract. It would not only bind Mary and Francis, but also provide closer links between the two countries in their opposition to England and the Reformation. Terms were agreed, and on 11 April 1558 an elaborate betrothal ceremony took place in the Louvre (D16) in Paris, then a royal palace. The festivities would have been particularly satisfying for members of the Guise family, as they saw Mary's future as the Dauphiness of France assured as preparations were made for the marriage.

The Louvre, like many other former royal palaces, is now a museum and one of the finest and richest in the world. It was the largest palace in Europe and the home to generations of French monarchs from the 14th century onwards. It was built over several centuries and recently a section of the massive wall of the original 12th-century keep was exposed to public view in the underground complex at the entrance to the museum. From the original building, Francis 1 began the construction of a new Renaissance palace which is now the enclosed Cour Carée. In 1528, Henry I began to move his court to Paris and set about refurbishing the Louvre.

The Louvre was given to the artists of France by Louis XIV and the Académie Française was housed there in 1672. Shortly after the Revolution, the Louvre was commandeered by the French authorities and was first opened as a museum in 1793. It contains a small bust of Mary Stuart which is regarded as an authentic likeness of her as a young girl in France. It is home to world-renowned works of art such as Leonardo de Vinci's Mona Lisa and the statues of Venus de Milo and Winged Victory of Samothrace. It would be interesting to know what some of those early artists might have thought of the 21m high glass pyramid which now graces the entrance to the museum.

On 24 April 1558, at the age of fifteen, Mary was married to Francis, who was nearly two years younger, in a lavish ceremony outside Notre Dame Cathedral in Paris.

Notre Dame Cathedral (D15) was started in 1163 when Gothic art was beginning to throw off the traditions of the Romanesque style and the building was completed 200 years later. The frontage has three great doorways. In the upper gallery are 28 statues of the kings of France. The West Front, before which Mary and Francis were married, with its magnificent rose window, was completed in the 13th century.

After the marriage ceremony outside, the royal couple proceeded into the church to celebrate Nuptial Mass. The honeymoon was spent at the château at Villers-Côtterets (D20) between Soissons and Meaux. (Villers-Côtterets was the birthplace, in 1802, of Alexandre Dumas, author of *The Three Musketeers*.)

*   *   *

In England meanwhile, changes had been taking place in both state and religious matters. After his death in 1547, Henry VIII had been succeeded by his son Edward VI who had only survived to reign for six years. There was then the very brief interlude of nine days when Lady Jane Grey took over the throne until Edward's half-sister, Mary Tudor, a staunch Roman Catholic, was crowned Queen in 1553, and the Church of Rome became the established religion once again. In 1558, the year that Mary Stuart and Francis were married, Queen Mary Tudor had died whilst negotiations were still taking place between Spain, France and England. These resulted in the Treaty of Cateau-Cambrésis in April 1559 between Henry II of France and Philip II of Spain. Due to the arguments about Elizabeth's illegitimacy and the change from Roman Catholicism to Protestantism in England, the Treaty brought about a re-assessment of the relationship between France and Spain with England and Scotland. From this agreement, a number of marriages were arranged including one between Princess Elisabeth of France and Philip II of Spain. In England, the Catholic star was fading and Protestantism was gaining ground. Elizabeth Tudor was proclaimed the new Queen of England.

CHAPTER 4

Queen Consort of France

IN THE EYES OF King Henry of France, his daughter-in-law, Mary Queen of Scots, was the rightful heir to the throne of England. His argument was the same as that of the Roman Catholic church – Elizabeth was illegitimate through the bigamous marriage of her father to Anne Boleyn. The French king at once insisted that Mary Stuart adopt the title of Queen of England together with the Arms of England quartered with those of France and Scotland on her royal canopy. This angered the English ambassador to France, Sir Nicholas Throckmorton, and he reported the matter to Queen Elizabeth. It was an early foundation for the stormy relationship between Queen Mary and Queen Elizabeth for years to come.

After Mary had married Francis, she found she had to spend longer periods of time in the presence of her mother-in-law, Queen Catherine de Medici. There was little similarity between the two women apart from their mutual concern over the increasing ill-health of the Dauphin. They were both well educated and there is little doubt there would have been some resentment born towards her daughter-in-law by Catherine. Mary was a beautiful young woman with auburn tresses. Catherine, according to portraits painted of her, was rather dumpy and plain. Altogether, she was not a very likeable personality which might be put down partly to her unhappy childhood. She had been orphaned at birth and had received little affection as a child in Florence. This had undoubtedly made her suspicious of others and rather unfeeling in her relationships with those around her. Her son, Francis, was unattractive, being a sallow youth and much smaller than Mary, and he had somewhat of a stoop when he walked.

In the following year of 1559, when the young Princess Elisabeth of France was betrothed to Philip II of Spain, the marriage was arranged by proxy as Philip was unable to make the journey. A number of celebrations were arranged to commemorate the event, and one of these was a jousting tournament which took place in Paris. Henry II of France was an enthusiastic jouster and decided to take part in the contest himself, dressed in black and white, the favourite colours of his mistress, Diane. He charged on horseback to face his third opponent, Montgomery, the commander of his Scottish guard. Montgomery thrust forward his lance and accidentally pierced the King's eye. Henry fell to the ground and, according to Lady Antonia Fraser, was carried off to the nearby Hôtel des Tournelles, situated in the Place Royale (now the Place de Vosges), where he lay unconscious for nine days. The dying monarch was watched over by Queen Catherine, Mary Stuart, Francis and other members of the royal family until his death.

King Henry II was buried at the Cathedral church at St Denis (D17) on 10 July 1559. Fifteen-year-old Francis became King of France and his wife, Mary Stuart, already Queen of Scots and claimant to the English throne, became Queen Consort. Members of the Guise family must have rubbed their hands together in glee at the news as they knew that their chance to seize power had arrived.

The Cathedral church at St Denis was the burial place of most of the French monarchs from Dagobert I to Louis XVIII over a span of twelve centuries. In 1793, permission was asked of the French Convention to destroy the tombs. They were subsequently pillaged and the human remains thrown into unmarked graves. Fortunately, some of the most precious funerary monuments were salvaged and removed to Paris. These are now kept at the Museum of French Monuments (from 1999 to be known as the Museum of Urban Heritage) at the Palais de Chaillot in the Place du Trocadèro. In 1816, some of the tombs were returned to the basilica at St

Denis by Louis XVIII including the monuments to Francis I, Catherine de Medici and Henry II.

According to legend, the evangelist Saint Denis, 1st Bishop of Lutetia, was beheaded in Montmartre and started to walk, carrying his head in his hands. He was buried where he fell by a saintly woman. An abbey was soon built on the site of his tomb and became a popular place for pilgrimage.

When King Henry II, died, it must have been a humiliating experience for Catherine de Medici to step down from her position as Queen Consort. She at once vented her fury on Diane de Poitiers and took back Chenonceau which Henry had presented to his mistress as a gift on his accession to the throne. As compensation, however, Catherine gave Chaumont to Diane.

Chenonceau (D5), situated on the River Cher, is one of the most picturesque and popular of all French châteaux. The original building was extended under the supervision of Diane. When Catherine de Medici took it back, she added the upper storeys to the five-arched bridge and extended the parkland. Between them they created a magnificent piece of architectural splendour. There is a long gallery 60m. in length paved with black and white squares. The Bedchamber of Five Queens has the coat of arms of five royal spouses, including those of Mary Stuart, above the bed. The chapel is entered through a carved door which has an inscription in English which is thought to date from the time of Mary. In the room of Francis I is a portrait of Diane de Poitiers called 'The Huntress, Diane', thought to have been painted by Primaticcio.

An avenue of plane trees leads up to the forecourt of the main part of the château. To the right are the extensive stables, built by Catherine, known as the Bâtiments de Domes which house a small wax museum with tableaux of Mary Stuart's marriage to the Dauphin and of her departure from France. Beyond the drawbridge is the 15th-century Tour des Marques. A second bridge crosses to the main building. As we face it, the garden of Catherine de Medici is to the right of the château and that of Diane de Poitiers to the left.

The château at Chaumont (D6) sits in a beautiful position, high on a cliff top above the Loire, and is approached from the nearby village. In the 1460s Charles d'Amboise inherited a feudal fortress and set about its transformation into a Renaissance château. There are a number of interesting rooms at Chaumont, some containing memorabilia connected with Catherine de Medici including a portrait of her when young. It was at Chaumont that an astrologer foretold the fate of Catherine de Medici's three sons of the House of Valois which became extinct in 1589, when the monarchy passed to the House of Bourbon. After Diane de Poitiers, the estate became the property of Jacques Le Ray who established a terracotta factory at the château. Nini set up a kiln there in 1772, and four years later, Benjamin Franklin, widely known as America's first citizen of the world, modelled for his sculpture in clay.

After the death of Henry II, preparations were soon in hand for the coronation of King Francis II which was to take place at Rheims Cathedral on 18 September 1559. Mary Stuart had already been crowned as an infant in Scotland, so there was no necessity for a double coronation to confirm her royal status. As the ceremony took place during the period of court mourning for Henry, proceedings were rather low-key with a minimum of pageantry and splendour.

Rheims (D21) is famous for two things in particular. One is the Cathedral and the other is its location at the centre of the champagne country. Its university was founded in 1547 by Mary Stuart's uncle, the Cardinal of Lorraine. The Cathedral was the traditional place for the coronation of most French monarchs up to Charles X in 1825.

The earliest building on the site of the Cathedral dates from the 5th century. This was destroyed by fire in 1210 and the present one was commenced the following year. The West Front has an array of sculptures and carvings and a beautiful rose window between twin towers. The interior has high nave vaulting, decorated with 13th-century statues. In the Lady Chapel is stained glass designed by Chagall, whilst on the walls hang several Flemish tapestries depicting the Life of the Virgin. The Cathedral, like much of the town, was severely damaged during the Second World War but has been lovingly restored.

Despite her loss of status in the royal household, Catherine de Medici continued to wield power in matters of state. Her son, Francis, the new King, was both unfit and unable to carry out his full responsibilities and much preferred to go hunting than attend to his official workload.

Mary, the Queen Consort, had other matters to consider. In France the French Protestants, known as the Huguenots, were regarded by King Henry II and the Cardinal of Lorraine as enemies of France and Rome. In Scotland, Protestantism was beginning to break new ground having found an ally in Queen Elizabeth. On Elizabeth's orders, a Treaty of Berwick was signed on 22 February 1560 between James Stewart, Mary's half-brother, Maitland of Lethington and herself. It specified that the Lords of the Congregation – supporters of the Protestant religion in Scotland – and the English should adopt a policy of mutual assistance against France. In essence, this promised English support for James Stewart and other Scottish nobles who had been opposing Mary of Guise and her Roman Catholic policies in Scotland. An army from England marched on Scotland to besiege the port of Leith, which had become the fortified home of Mary of Guise and her court as well as being the headquarters for Scottish troops and their French allies.

Meanwhile, in France the Cardinal of Lorraine and the 2nd Duke of Guise had tightened their grip on both political and religious affairs, especially since infiltration by the Huguenots. In 1560 this body had planned a large uprising and their idea was to seize King Francis and his Queen, Mary Stuart, and remove them from the over-dominant influence of the Guises who, by now, were ruling France from behind the throne. This boded ill for religious tolerance. The coup was to take place at Blois (D8), but the Guises got wind of the plan and swiftly moved the court to Amboise (D4), a walled stronghold. The conspirators were rounded up and were either beheaded or hung from a balustrade at Amboise. This balustrade is now known as the Conspirators Balcony.

There had been a château at Amboise since 496 AD and it became a royal residence in 1434 under Charles VII. From 1492 on it was completely rebuilt by ensuing monarchs and continued to be occupied by the royal family until 1560. In 1515, Leonardo da Vinci was invited by Francis I to help him with the decoration at Amboise as well as Chambord and he also helped to arrange sumptuous banquets for the King. He stayed in the small 15th-century manor house, Château Clos-Lucé, and died there in 1519. His remains are reputedly buried in the chapel of St Hubert.

When the stench of decaying bodies at Amboise became unbearable, it ceased to be used as a royal residence. It was later used as a state prison. It is the only royal palace which belongs to the Prince of Paris, the present claimant to the throne of France.

Mary suffered a devastating blow when news arrived from Scotland that her mother, Mary of Guise, weary with the constant burden of six years of Regency, had died of dropsy at Edinburgh Castle (A1) on 11 June 1560. The young Queen was inconsolable. It was agreed that her mother should be buried in France, but it was not until March 1561 that her body was brought from Scotland by boat. It had probably lain for some time in St Margaret's Chapel in Edinburgh Castle before being smuggled on board ship for passage to France.

The body was first taken to Fècamp Abbey (D28) in Normandy. The abbey church of La Trinité at Fècamp dates from the 12th century and is one of France's largest Gothic churches. Among many interesting features in the vaulted Norman Gothic interior is the Sanctuary of the Precious Blood. According to legend, a mysterious boat bearing a few drops of Christ's blood collected by Joseph of Arimathea in a lead container, was pushed out to sea and landed at Fècamp in the 1st century. The phial is now kept in a marble tabernacle at the rear of the high altar. The remains of the original Abbey are in the rue des Fortes. The buildings house the former Benedictine distillery and a museum about the history and work of the Abbey.

Mary of Guise's remains were then taken to Rheims for interment at the Benedictine Abbey of St Pierre where Mary of Guise's sister, Renée, was Mother Abbess at the Convent. Sadly, a full-length bronze monument of Mary of Guise was destroyed during the French Revolution. Nothing now remains of the Abbey.

On 6 July 1560 a Treaty of Edinburgh was completed between Queen Elizabeth and purported representatives of Francis and Mary Stuart. This specified that the royal couple would no longer jointly lay claim to the throne of England but recognise Elizabeth as Queen. The agreement also stated that both French and English forces would withdraw from Scotland. However, the arrangement was never confirmed by Mary and she refused to agree to any communication that had taken place without her own specific approval or that of her Privy Council. The terms of the agreement were never carried out.

For Mary Stuart, it had been bad enough losing her father-in-law and then her own mother, but the young Queen was to need every ounce of courage when King Francis returned from hunting one day in Orléans (D9) and complained of a violent pain in his ear. Despite gentle nursing by Mary and his mother in the Hôtel Groslot, which was used as the royal residence when the monarch visited Orléans, the king's condition worsened. The growth in his ear soon spread to his brain. He died on 5 December 1560 and had reigned for just seventeen months.

Orléans is famed for its links with Joan of Arc (1412 - 31) who was born at Domremy-la-Pucelle. As a young maid still in her teens, she led an army into Orléans on 29 April 1429 in the wake of occupying English troops. Joan managed to raise the siege within eight days, a feat which influenced the outcome of the War between France and England. She went on to free other centres but was eventually condemned as a heretic by a court of French clerics. She was burnt at the stake in Rouen on 30 May 1431. In the early 20th century Joan of Arc was elevated to sainthood. An equestrian statue of her stands in the Place du Martroi in Orléans.

The Hôtel Groslot in Orléans, where Francis died, is now the

Hôtel de Ville. It is a large Renaissance building built by a merchant, Jacques Groslot, and dates from 1530. The two matching wings were added in 1790 when it became the town hall. In front of the building is another statue of Joan of Arc, standing in meditation; it is a replica of an original in marble at Versailles.

Mary Queen of Scots, Queen Consort of France, had become a widow at only eighteen years of age. Francis was succeeded as King by his brother, Charles IX, as Mary went into mourning which was to last for forty days. On 18 January 1561, Mary travelled to Orléans to attend a memorial service to Francis at the Convent of Grey Friars. Now the Dowager Queen, her presence at court had become of no real consequence. Catherine de Medici assumed power once again in the role of Regent for her son, Charles. The Guises began to lose control over the affairs of state as their power started to diminish. Charles IX only lived a short time, but Catherine's influence at court continued when her youngest son, Henry III, inherited the crown.

It was not long before it was suggested that Mary should re-marry. Don Carlos, son and heir to the throne of Spain, was considered. This would have meant that his father, Philip II, would have to commit his country to the possibility of financing Scottish campaigns against England and the idea did not appeal to him. Catherine did not wish to see Mary marry Don Carlos as her own daughter, Princess Elisabeth, was by now Philip II's third wife. Neither would she allow Mary to marry her second son, Charles.

Another alternative was open to Mary. She could return to Scotland to take up her duties as Queen of Scots despite the difficulties which might lie ahead. At least she could be an independent monarch without interference from the Guise family or her mother-in-law.

Whilst considering the situation, Mary decided to visit some of her Guise relatives and set off for Rheims to see her mother's burial place at the Convent of St Pierre and visit her aunt, the Mother Abbess. The next member of her family she wished to see was her uncle Charles, Cardinal of Lorraine, at Nancy. However, en route, she stopped off at the fortress of Vitry-le-Francois (D22), which had been built by Francis I in 1545. (It was dismantled in the 19th century.) It was here that she had a meeting with John Leslie, Bishop of Ross, to discuss her possible return to Scotland. The Bishop's advice was that if she came back to Scotland, she should land at Aberdeen. He assured Mary that there would be an army waiting to fight her cause against the Protestant lords, who had caused her mother so much heartache during her Regency. Mary did not respond to his suggestion.

Mary then met Lord James Stewart at St Dizier (D23), and discussed with him the possible arrangements for her return to Scotland. By this time, she had made up her mind that she wanted to go back to the country of her birth. James was now thirty, twelve years older than his royal half-sister. If he had not been born on 'the wrong side of the blanket', he would have been the automatic successor to James V. This fact had always frustrated him and he resented Mary's lifestyle and position as the product of a legitimate marriage. During their discussions James explained some of the changes that had taken place in Scotland during her absence. He asked her to renounce the Catholic church in favour of the Protestant faith. She refused and, knowing of his support for the Reformation, offered to make him a cardinal if he himself would renounce the new religion. He in turn turned down Mary's proposal. He went on to explain that if she was unwilling to forego her Catholic beliefs, then she must accept the Protestant church and confine her religious activities to private worship. Clearly Mary knew that she had problems ahead when she returned.

At Nancy she discussed the situation with the Cardinal of Lorraine who would obviously have given her strict instructions to stand up to her principles regarding the Catholic faith. No doubt he had learned much from his sister, Mary of Guise, about the affairs of Scotland and this he would have related to his niece.

Nancy (D25) is the historic capital of Lorraine and the château had been one of the principal seats of the Guise family since the 12th century. The town was much improved by Henry, 3rd Duke of Guise (1545-1608). Adjoining the Palais de Gouvernement is the former ducal palace, a Gothic building begun in 1495 by Renè II and continued by his son, Antoine, whose equestrian statue surmounts the gateway. The surviving wing, restored after a fire in 1871, contains the Museum of Lorraine History, one of the most interesting provincial collections of its kind in France.

After visiting her uncle and aunt, the 2nd Duke and Duchess of Guise, Mary returned to Rheims and was re-united with her aunt Renée and other relatives at the Abbey of St Pierre. Mary then returned to the French court to start making the necessary arrangements for her journey. She sent a letter to Elizabeth through an emissary requesting safe conduct through England. As the Queen of Scots had not ratified the Treaty of Edinburgh recognising Elizabeth as Queen of England, Elizabeth was furious and refused to grant the petition.

Mary took leave of her relatives at the French court and departed from St Germain (D12) bound for the port of Calais (D29). Her final journey in France took her via Beauvais (D26), which has a fine cathedral where the reconstructed choir is the highest Gothic vault in existence. Most of the 15th-and 16th-century buildings were destroyed during the Second World War. She made her next stop at Abbeville (D27). It was here in 1514 that Mary Tudor, sister of Henry VIII, had married Louis XII of France in the Church of St Vulfrun. King Louis died just three months after his marriage to the English princess. The central part of the decorative west front of the church contains a lion rampant with the royal arms, symbolising the linking of France with England by the marriage. Abbeville also suffered extensive damage in the Second World War.

Mary and her entourage, which included two of her uncles, the 2nd Duke of Guise and the Cardinal of Lorraine, both of whom were to accompany their niece to Scotland, finally arrived at Calais. Calais played a prominent role in the struggles between England and France. The port was taken by Edward III in 1347 and remained in English hands until 1558 when its garrison was

Dumbarton Castle
Mary embarked for France from Dumbarton Castle in
August 1548 when only five years old.

Inverness from Tomnhurich
The Queen of Scots was refused entry to Inverness Castle by the Governor on her first visit in 1562. He was later hanged.

Edinburgh Castle
Mary gave birth to her son and heir, Prince James, in the Castle. He became James VI of Scotland when his mother was forced to abdicate in his favour in 1567.

Carlisle Castle
Mary's first English prison where she was held for six weeks before being moved to Bolton Castle.

Chartley Manor
Mary's prison in Staffordshire where the Babington Plot was uncovered.

Glamis Castle
Mary visited the Castle during her Royal Progress to the
North East in August 1562.

Ruins of St Andrew's Castle
Scene of Cardinal Beaton's murder in 1546. The Castle was captured
by French troops the following year when John Knox was taken
prisoner to France.

expelled by the Duke of Guise at the head of 30,000 troops. This proved a major humiliation for Queen Mary Tudor during her short reign as Queen of England. At the time, she was reported to have made the statement, 'When I die, you shall find Calais written upon my heart!'

It was in Calais that a nobleman from the Scottish border country first entered Mary's life. James Hepburn, 4th Earl of Bothwell, arrived to act as admiral of the fleet of galleys and steer them past hostile English ships in the English Channel and North Sea. Although he was committed to reform, Bothwell had been an ally of Mary's mother and was against the English. His character had been much influenced by his uncle, Patrick Hepburn, Bishop of Moray, who was noted for his immorality.

Whilst awaiting suitable weather to sail to Scotland, Mary Stuart and her party would have stayed at another of the Guise mansions. Finally, on 14 August 1561, Queen Mary stepped on board the galley which was to take her with her supporters and servants back to her native country. Even though it was August, there was a heavy mist. As the boat pulled out, she could only gaze back and ponder on her happy years in France. Uppermost in her mind as she sailed off to an uncertain future must have been the thought, 'Will I ever return?'

CHAPTER 5

Scotland Again

THE GALLEYS SAILED ACROSS the English Channel and into the North Sea heading for Scotland. Although they were pursued by English ships, these kept a discreet distance and did not interfere. Five days after leaving France, the boats headed into the Firth of Forth. It was a misty day when they arrived at the port of Leith (B1) and dropped anchor in the harbour. Leith had been transformed into a fortified town by Mary of Guise during her Regency, and from 1548 the town withstood siege by Protestant Lords until early in 1560. As well as being a commercial centre in its own right, it had for hundreds of years been the port for Edinburgh. Today, it is home to the royal yacht, *Britannia*, berthed in Leith after it came to the end of its life as a sea-going vessel.

Mary Stuart expected there would be a guard of honour and full ceremonial awaiting her arrival, but the royal party docked earlier than expected and there was no official person to welcome her back to Scotland. She was conducted to the house of Andrew

Edinburgh Castle

Lamb (B1), a local merchant who owned a substantial property just off the quayside. The house is still there and the exterior can be viewed. Mary was given refreshment and entertained while preparations were made for her to leave for the Palace of Holyroodhouse. News quickly spread of the Queen's arrival and the townsfolk turned out to give her a warm welcome. She was eighteen years old, almost six feet tall, and her grace and beauty immediately endeared her to the people. Initially, Mary was to prove a very popular monarch. She was greeted by her half-brother, James Stewart, Maitland of Lethington, Châtelherault, and other officials who came to Leith as representatives of the Scottish Parliament to accompany her to Holyrood.

On arrival at the Palace of Holyroodhouse (A8), Mary was conducted to her apartments in the north-west tower which had been much altered during the reign of her father, James V. Additional Renaissance work had also been incorporated which would remind Mary of some of the châteaux she had left behind in France.

The Palace of Holyroodhouse is situated just beneath Salisbury Crags and the extinct volcano known as Arthur's Seat which provide an energetic climb for the fit walker. The views over the city of Edinburgh and across the Forth estuary and beyond are magnificent. It is perhaps best to do the climb early in the day when the sleeping town is just beginning to stir beneath the morning mist which sometimes hovers around the Castle Rock. Another good time is on a sunny evening when the dramatic outline of the Castle and its precincts stands out against a glowing skyline of distant towers, pinnacles, spires, hills and mountains away to the west.

The Palace of Holyroodhouse already had a turbulent history before Mary arrived. The adjacent Holyrood Abbey (A9) was founded by King David I of Scotland in 1128. According to legend, the King founded the Abbey on the spot where, whilst hunting on the day of the Holy Rood, he saw a vision of the Holy Cross which appeared in his hands as he was about to be gored by a stag. An Augustinian community of monks was established and after about sixty years a larger building was constructed. When wars with England began, the Abbey suffered greatly. In particular, the attacks during the Rough Wooing of Henry VIII in the 1540s caused massive desecration of the monastic place of worship.

The earliest buildings of the Palace of Holyroodhouse were started around the cloisters of the Abbey between 1501 and 1505 by James IV in anticipation of his marriage to Margaret Tudor in 1503. Further work was carried out by his son, James V, between 1528 and 1532. It was a single tower residence until other parts were added to extend the premises along the western side of the square. The north-west tower will forever be associated with the Queen of Scots and the dastardly murder of her Italian Secretary, David Rizzio. After Mary's time, the Palace of Holyroodhouse continued to be a favourite with her son, James VI, but once having acceded to the English throne in 1603, he only paid one more visit there. The Scottish Coronation of his son, Charles I, took place in Holyrood Abbey, and extensive work had to be carried out to accommodate the ceremony. There was a disastrous fire in 1650 when some of Oliver Cromwell's forces were stationed at the Palace. Cromwell ordered repairs to the damage.

By the time the monarchy was restored in 1660, Holyroodhouse had again become an official royal residence under Charles II. Three sides of the main quadrangle were reconstructed in 1671. From then on, Holyroodhouse as a royal place of residence fell in and out of favour with different monarchs. In 1745, Prince Charles Edward Stuart stayed there during the early days of the Uprising in an attempt to reclaim the throne for his father. In 1795, following the French Revolution, the Royal Apartments were occupied by the Comte d'Artois, brother of Louis XVI, and subsequently by the deposed King Charles X of France. It was not until 1822 that the Palace came to prominence again when George IV was invited to visit Scotland. Gradually, the place was brought back to a habitable condition. Queen Victoria used it more as a convenient place to stop over rather than a royal residence. She much preferred the beautiful setting and solitude of Balmoral Castle on Deeside. Today, the Palace of Holyroodhouse regularly serves as an official home for Queen Elizabeth II and other members of the royal family when they are in Scotland. With its colourful and often bloody background, it has become one of Scotland's most popular visitor attractions.

Standing outwith the grounds of Holyroodhouse – close to the bottom of The Royal Mile in Abbeyhill – is a quaint little building known as Queen Mary's Bath House. It is reputed that the Queen bathed herself there in white wine to preserve her beauty. At the end of the 18th century a richly inlaid dagger was found under the slates of the roof. It was thought, with some reason, that it may have belonged to one of the murderers of the Queen's favourite, David Rizzio.

Once Mary Queen of Scots had been installed at Holyroodhouse for a few days, she, her ladies, and her French servants realised that the mood at the Scottish court was much more solemn than the court in France. There was far less frivolity, dancing and music, and the attitude of courtiers was serious in the extreme. In addition, after the Rough Wooing in the 1540s, the Palace had not recovered from the wanton destruction and theft of much of its contents. Queen Mary therefore used her income from France to restore and beautify the property to make it a suitable court residence.

Soon after her arrival, the Queen made her first official entry into Edinburgh. She received an enthusiastic welcome from the citizens as she rode up the High Street which had been festooned and decorated for the occasion. Gunfire sounded from the Castle and the noise of merrymaking rang around the streets. There were speeches, pageants and singing by children, creating a memorable day in Mary's life. But things would soon begin to alter, as even though she had only been away from Scotland for just over thirteen years, great changes had taken place, especially in the religious sphere.

During her mother's Regency, Protestantism had more or less

taken over as the religion in Scotland. This was especially welcomed by the English court which had given support and encouragement to those Scottish lords and others who were converts to the new faith. Some were hardened bigots, none more so than their leader, John Knox, a fiery preacher who ruled his church with a rod of iron. He was to become one of Mary's most bitter enemies.

John Knox was born in 1514 in Haddington at, according to tradition, the Gifford Gate, a local thoroughfare. He trained to become a priest but found himself without a job. He then worked as a notary and as a private tutor to wealthy families. It was whilst he was working in East Lothian that he met the Reformer, George Wishart, who encouraged him to work towards the reform of the established Roman Catholic Church. He became Wishart's bodyguard until the latter was arrested and put to death. Knox avoided this fate and joined other Reformers to avenge the murder of his mentor. From the pulpit of the parish church of St Andrews (B32), Knox preached a powerful sermon in which he incited the citizens of St Andrews and local lords to take the Archbishop's Castle and murder Cardinal Beaton who had been responsible for the burning of many Protestant heretics. Knox and other Reformers succeeded in holding the castle against Mary of Guise's French guard for a year. When in 1547 the French finally stormed the castle, Knox was taken away as a prisoner to Nantes (D3) in France and made to serve as a galley slave for nineteen months. Most of his companions died in slavery but he survived, though badly traumatised by the experience.

On his release, Knox went to England and was well received. He became minister of the church in Berwick-upon-Tweed where he could keep his ears open as to what was happening in Scottish religious affairs. News of his preaching soon reached London and he was invited to become a royal chaplain.

However, on the accession of Mary Tudor in 1553, all known Protestants in England were put to death, so Knox fled to the Continent. He travelled as far as Geneva where he became an ardent follower of John Calvin, an architect of the Reformation who was a great Protestant idealist and an important leader of the Reformed religion.

Knox returned to Scotland on a temporary basis in 1555 and was responsible for recruiting many new converts to the Reformed Church. In 1559, he preached such an impassioned sermon in St John's Kirk in Perth (B44) that some 6,000 Protestants ransacked the town looking for Catholic images to destroy. He soon became a powerful force in Scotland and was convinced he was God's disciple sent to overthrow the papist religion. Knox had strong support from many Scottish nobles who had formed themselves into a body called the Lords of the Congregation. Thus, Mary arrived back in Scotland when these revolutionary changes had already taken place through an Act of Parliament in 1560. John Knox was based in Edinburgh at the High Kirk of St Giles (A2) in the High Street. Despite his bigoted approach to religious matters, he had a streak of hypocrisy in him. In middle age he had, in succession, married a sixteen-year-old girl then one of seventeen. A classic male chauvinist, he strongly objected to any woman in authority over men. His violent opposition to Mary Stuart and the 'frivolous' behaviour of her court was therefore not unexpected.

A church had stood on the site of St Giles since the 9th century. It was burnt down in 1385 during an invasion by the English. Rebuilding work commenced during the 15th century and included the crown spire, an extension to the church, raising the rafters, and the addition of clerestory windows and five chapels, one of which is now the Thistle Chapel established in 1911. This is the chapel of the Knights of the Thistle, holders of Scotland's premier order of chivalry awarded by the Sovereign. During the Reformation, St Giles became a hotbed of Calvinism through the preachings and activities of Knox and his followers. It was elevated to the status of cathedral during the reign of James VI.

Further down the High Street, on the opposite side from St Giles, is John Knox's House (A6). The building dates from around 1490 and is a typical town house. Knox is reputed to have lived there between the years 1561 and 1572. In 1853, after restoration and refurbishment had been carried out, it was turned into a museum about the life and achievements of the great preacher and advocate of the Reformed Church.

A statue of John Knox stands in the Quadrangle of New College at the Church of Scotland General Assembly Hall at the top of The Mound in Edinburgh. This building stands on the site of the palace of Mary of Guise. There is also a statue of Knox in Haddington, at the Knox Memorial Institute (now a centre for the elderly) in Knox Place.

Religion was not the only problem facing Queen Mary on her return to Scotland. The political situation was plagued by family disagreements and rivalries between various lords, a number of whom were related to Mary Stuart. Much of the unrest was due to their lust for power, property and land. It was often the case that a dishonoured noble would be relieved of his lands and possessions by the monarch. Equally, a nobleman could be rewarded if, in the opinion of the sovereign, he had served the crown well by his actions. In particular, the bestowal and removal of titles by the monarch was much in evidence at this time in history. Queen Mary was no exception and she occasionally stripped people of their rank and possessions if they had crossed or opposed her in some way. Equally, she conferred titles and lands on those who pleased her or of whom she was fond.

Mary knew about some of the changes that had taken place in her absence. She had already discussed the situation with James Stewart when they met in France. A leading Protestant, he was receiving financial help from England in an effort to enhance the new faith in Scotland. Mary had agreed to consider recognising the newly established religion but insisted on her right to practice her own and this had been accepted by him. Problems with saying Mass at Holyrood Abbey arose on the very first Sunday after Mary's arrival. Only the actions of James probably prevented the Reformers from forcing entry to the Abbey. Even at that early stage, the Queen had come to be reliant upon her half-brother for advice and support in her new surroundings. News that Holyrood Abbey was being used to celebrate Mass soon reached the ears of John Knox and he raised a strong objection. The only thing to be done was for Mary to hold an interview with Knox to sort out the matter once and for all. This was the beginning of an uncomfortable and stormy relationship.

From the start of the discussion it was obvious that Knox would make no allowances for Queen Mary's own form of worship. The conversation soon became a sermon which he preached at the Queen, urging her to abandon her ways lest she become tainted further by the idolatry of popery. For Knox there was no compromise. His words were powerful and passionate in the extreme.

At every opportunity Knox continued in his mission to criticise and condemn Mary, branding her from the pulpit the 'Whore of Babylon'. He remained a constant threat to Mary's personal happiness for years to come. James Stewart, a supporter of John Knox, urged the Queen to accept the new religion publicly and only follow the Roman Catholic form of service in private. Queen Mary still found this hard to accept.

After some weeks, in order to get away from Edinburgh and the rantings of Knox and to make herself known to her subjects, Mary decided to follow a royal progress around part of her kingdom. She was to make a number of progresses over the next few years in an effort to consolidate support. On 10 August 1561, the Queen set off for her birthplace at Linlithgow Palace (B18). It was a nostalgic visit and she was greeted by her subjects as she rode through the town and climbed the hill into the rambling building. Two days later, Mary went on to Stirling Castle (B25) where she had lived during her early childhood.

The party then continued to Leslie Castle (B37) and Perth (B44) where, apart from some anti-Catholic demonstrations, the Queen was given a warm welcome. She had been invited to Leslie Castle by John Leslie, 5th Earl of Rothes, who was a leading member of the Lords of the Congregation and had been an enemy of

Mary of Guise. He was to become a member of the Privy Council. John Leslie was Bishop of Ross and later became Mary's envoy during her captive years in England.

The entourage moved from Perth to Dundee (B45) where, on a later visit in 1564, the Queen presented a piece of land – The Howff – to the citizens, which has since been used as a burial ground. Mary reputedly stayed at a dwelling which once stood at the corner of Church Lane and Thorter Row. She then crossed the River Tay to Earlshall Castle (B33), near Leuchars, where she stayed to enjoy the hunting.

Earlshall Castle is famed for the topiary in its magnificent gardens. Built by Sir William Bruce in 1546, by the late 19th century it was fast falling into disrepair. It was taken on in 1890 by a new owner, Robert Mackenzie, who set about the restoration of the castle and planning of the gardens. The Long Gallery has a magnificent coved, heraldic painted ceiling and it is easy to feel the spirit of Mary moving along its welcoming corridors and staircases to the Great Hall.

From Earlshall, it was only a short journey to St Andrews. During the early Middle Ages, a legend arose that the relics of St Andrew had been brought to Scotland. Remains of the saints were thought to be a link between heaven and earth and were therefore greatly revered by the established church of Rome. As a result, the town and cathedral at St Andrews soon became the most important centre for pilgrimages in Western Europe.

Mary Stuart visited the magnificent Cathedral (B32) in which her parents had been married. The Cathedral was founded in 1160, became the largest in the country, and was completed in 1318. After sermons delivered by John Knox in 1559, a certain amount of destruction of ornaments took place. Knox was following the doctrines of John Calvin that the cult of saints and the veneration of human remains should be discontinued. He urged his followers to rid all churches of such idolatry. By 1649 St Andrews Cathedral had been reduced to a state of ruin. Nonetheless, we can still surmise from what remains just how large the great church must have been, especially in the length of the nave.

The University of St Andrews, founded in 1412, is the oldest in Scotland and includes three colleges and a number of historic buildings. The United Colleges of St Salvator and St Leonard, founded in 1450 and 1512, are famous for the Church of St Salvator, now the College Chapel. It contains the tomb of its founder, Bishop Kennedy, John Knox's pulpit, and the oldest Sacrament House in a Scottish Church. The United Colleges now worship together in this church. One of the other Colleges, St Mary's, was founded in 1538 by Cardinal Beaton. There is a quadrangle between the older buildings where a hawthorn tree planted by Mary Queen of Scots still grows. There are also some remains of the original St Leonard's College in which John Knox resided, and nearby is the small St Leonard's Chapel. In the grounds of St Madras College stands the Blackfriars Chapel dating from 1525, a fragment of the monastery founded originally in 1274.

The town church, Holy Trinity, was founded in 1412 and, though much altered, retains its 16th-century tower. Knox preached his first public sermon in this building in 1547. A house in South Street, built by Hugh Scrymgeour in 1523 and now part of St Leonard's School for Girls, is said to be where Mary stayed during her visits to St Andrews. However, it is more likely that she resided at the Palace within the monastic complex of the Cathedral.

The ruined St Andrews Castle stands on a rock overlooking the sea and was founded in 1200. It was here that Cardinal Beaton was murdered in 1546 and John Knox was taken prisoner and sent to the galleys. Notable features include a 24ft deep bottle-dungeon and, to the south-east of the courtyard, an underground passage made during the siege which followed the murder of Beaton.

St Andrews is perhaps best known as the home of golf. The Old Course dates back to the 15th century and near to the Club House of the Royal and Ancient is the Martyrs Monument which commemorates some of the reformers who were burnt at St

Andrews in the 15th and 16th centuries. Mary Queen of Scots is reputed to have played 'goff' during at least one of her visits to the town.

Mary and her party moved on to Falkland Palace (B36) where she may have played tennis in the gardens which contain the Royal Tennis Court, built in 1539, the oldest in Britain. Mary would also have enjoyed hunting and riding in the nearby Lomond Hills which overlook this former residence of the Stewart kings and queens. After a brief stay at Falkland, the return journey to Edinburgh was by boat across the Firth of Forth – there were no Forth Bridges in those days – from North Queensferry (B28) to the port of Leith (B1) and thence back to Holyroodhouse. Apart from a few demonstrations, the tour had been very successful and endeared Mary to many of her subjects whom she had met along the way. Undoubtedly, this first royal progress would have given her much greater insight into the religious situation in Scotland. She needed to show that she was in support of the Protestant faith, contrary though it might be to her own beliefs.

Mary's closest confidants were James Stewart and her Secretary, William Maitland of Lethington. Her personal interests included needlework, music and dancing. She also played the lute and wrote poetry. It was through Mary's love of music that the name David Rizzio first came to her attention. He worked for the Ambassador for Savoy and volunteered his services to the court choir during his stay. Mary was enchanted with his voice and music and Rizzio soon found himself being drawn into court life in close proximity to the Queen. She quickly came to depend on him in many ways.

Generally, matters were working quite well for Mary. She felt Queen Elizabeth of England might be lenient towards her and perhaps more supportive of her claim to be her successor to the English throne. Yet Elizabeth could not dismiss from her mind what had happened in France when Mary had been proclaimed Queen of England. Mary insisted that the quartering of the English Arms over her canopy was the work of her father-in-law,

King Henry II, but suspicion obviously still lingered, especially when Elizabeth enquired whether Mary Stuart had yet put her name to the Treaty of Edinburgh. Despite this, the Queen of Scots persisted in her correspondence with Elizabeth and sent emissaries to the English court in an effort to build up a closer relationship. At one stage, it seemed Elizabeth might be willing to meet face to face with Mary. Discussions took place regarding the possibility of the two Queens having audience with one another in York. However, Elizabeth withdrew from the idea when she learned that war had broken out in France between the Huguenots and the Catholics. She had no wish to upset her own Protestant subjects if it became known that she had collaborated with the Catholic Queen of Scots.

Mary's second royal progress, which began in August 1562, was aimed at visiting some of the north-eastern parts of her kingdom. She was encouraged to do this by James Stewart. It would involve her going to Aberdeen (B52) which would be convenient because it was close to the lands and property of Mary's cousin, George Gordon, 4th Earl of Huntly, who was also a Catholic. Known as 'Cock o' the North', he had become an over-powerful force in Scottish politics which had chilled his relationship with Mary since she had arrived back in Scotland. Neither did he see eye to eye with Lord James Stewart.

Close to Huntly's territory were lands which had formerly been held by the Earls of Moray, a title which had lapsed. Huntly had taken upon himself the task of administering these estates, extracting appropriate incomes and living a lavish lifestyle. Mary was persuaded by James Stewart to confer the title and its associated benefits upon himself. Huntly had yet to be informed and this was a confrontation she would not be savouring.

From Edinburgh, the royal party proceeded to Stirling (B25) then on to Perth (B44), heading eastwards through Coupar Angus to Glamis Castle (B48).

Glamis Castle is situated in the Vale of Strathmore and has

been in the possession of the Lyon family since 1372 when Sir John Lyon married Joanna, daughter of King Robert II. Macbeth was Thane of Glamis and the place was a popular royal hunting lodge between the 11th and 14th centuries. James V and his Queen held court there. Much later, it was the childhood home of Lady Elizabeth Bowes-Lyon, Queen Elizabeth, The Queen Mother. Her younger daughter, Princess Margaret, was born at Glamis in 1930, the first royal princess to be born in Scotland for over 300 years. The Castle is one of the most beautiful in Scotland. The greater part of the structure dates from 1675-87 but an older tower, with 15-ft thick walls, has survived. The Castle is the seat of the Earl of Strathmore and Kinghorne and has the reputation of being one of the most haunted in the whole of Scotland.

Mary Stuart is reported to have enjoyed herself at Glamis on her short visit, and a menu written in French, has been preserved, from her stay there.

She next went to Edzell Castle (B50), once the largest castle in the county of Forfar but now a ruin. The most remarkable feature is the walled garden, dating from 1604, with its intriguing square recesses in the walls. It has a bower which was used by Mary Queen of Scots, and a turreted garden-house has also survived.

From Edzell, the next point of call was Dunnottar Castle (B51), set in a dramatic location on a headland overlooking the North Sea. It was built in the 14th century and was the home of the Earl Marischal, Sir William Keith. Scenes from Zeffirelli's film of Shakespeare's *Hamlet* were shot at Dunnottar.

Mary then moved on to Aberdeen (B52) where she arrived on 27 August 1562. She mainly wished to see Huntly, but made time to visit the University as well as hold court. The situation had become tense as Lord Huntly was a staunch critic of Queen Mary. His son, Sir John Gordon, had been involved in an Edinburgh scuffle. He had been imprisoned, but escaped and his mother, Lady Huntly, met the Queen to plead mercy on her son's behalf. Mary suggested he first return to gaol. This he did but soon escaped again, only to summon up military assistance to attack the royal party as they continued on their travels heading for Inverness (B60).

The Queen called at Darnaway Castle near Forres (B58), a stronghold of the former Earls of Moray, where she proclaimed James Stewart as the new Earl. The ruined Darnaway Castle of today still retains the 15th-century hall of an earlier structure. The scenery in the valley to the south, where the river flows between the forest and the woods of Altyre, is of exceptional beauty. By tradition, the three witches whom Macbeth stumbled upon in Shakespeare's play were supposed to have met on a heath outside the nearby town of Forres.

On her arrival at Inverness Castle (B60), Mary was refused entry by the Keeper, another of Huntly's sons. This was considered an act of treason as the building was a royal property. Lord Huntly soon discovered that local townsfolk were rallying support for Mary and immediately sent word to his son to allow admission.

The Inverness Castle of Mary's day was not on the same site as the present building which overlooks the River Ness. It was situated at the point where General Wade built his barracks, called Fort George, at the northern terminal of two great military roads built in the 18th century. After the destruction of Fort George by Prince Charles Edward Stuart in 1746, a new Fort George was built to the north-east on a spit of land overlooking the Moray Firth. According to tradition, the house where Mary stayed in the town of Inverness whilst awaiting entry to the Castle was in Bridge Street.

After a few days of relative calm in Inverness, the royal entourage set off again for Aberdeen. The first stop, on 15 September, was at Kilravock Castle (B59), the ancestral home of the Ross clan, situated on the northern side of the valley of the River Nairn. It was built in 1460 and the present castle incorporates the original tall keep within the 17th-century manor house. Politically, Lord Kilravock did not commit himself to the new Protestant leadership in Edinburgh and he received Mary at his castle. Her room was in the vaulted fourth floor of the keep.

Continuing on their journey back to Aberdeen (B52), a call was made at Spynie Palace near Elgin (B57). The site of Spynie Palace, now in ruins, is dominated by a massive tower built by Bishop David Stewart and affords splendid views across nearby Spynie Loch. It was once a childhood home of the Earl of Bothwell whose great-uncle was Bishop of Moray at the time of Queen Mary's visit. (It was to him that Bothwell would later go after his escape from Carberry Hill prior to his flight to Scandinavia.)

The next call was at the 13th-century Balvenie Castle near Dufftown (B55), an Atholl stronghold, which was extended in the 15th and 16th centuries. Originally the property of the Comyns, Edward I of England visited the site in 1304. The moated building with a curtain wall is set in a picturesque location.

Queen Mary was still being pursued on her travels by Huntly's son, Sir John Gordon. News was also received that Lord Huntly himself was beginning to build up forces of his own for some sort of attack. He followed her with his troops and matters came to a climax when he was out-flanked by the Queen's supporters. However, rather than submit to them, Huntly chose to fight. At the battle of Corrichie (B53), nineteen kilometres west of Aberdeen, his troops were defeated by James Stewart, the new Earl of Moray. Huntly fell from his horse and died. A massive granite pillar in a roadside clearing off the B977, which skirts the south-eastern flank of the Hill of Fare, commemorates the site of the battle. Huntly was eventually laid to rest at Elgin Cathedral (B56) after a gruesome ritual had first been performed, which included the corpse being taken to Edinburgh and tried before Parliament for high treason.

Mary arrived back in Aberdeen on 22 September. Huntly's son, Sir John Gordon, was executed there, and the Queen was forced to watch the proceedings by her half-brother, Moray. This act took place at the Old Tollbooth which has been part of the Town House since 1868.

Huntly Castle was confiscated, but eventually Mary was to restore the estates to Huntly's second son and heir, George Gordon, the 5th Earl. After the battle, he had fled to his father-in-law, the Duke of Châtelherault, but was later placed in custody at Dunbar and convicted of treason in February 1563. He might easily have been put to death and it was only his long association with Queen Mary which saved him. He stayed in jail until after the marriage of Mary to Darnley when it became necessary for her to rally support against the rebels in their bid for Protestant supremacy and their opposition to her marriage. George Gordon became one of the Queen's most loyal supporters and closest allies. His sister, Jean Gordon, was the first wife of the 4th Earl of Bothwell.

Huntly Castle (B54), close to the town of Huntly, had been re-built by the 4th Earl of Huntly following his visit to France with Mary of Guise in 1566. It is set in a lovely riverside location and is famed for its fine heraldic sculpture and inscribed stone friezes.

Mary decided to make her way back to Edinburgh and continued her journey down the East Coast paying her second visit to Dunnottar Castle (B51). Following the coastline, she next stayed at Arbroath, most probably in the Abbot's House which dates from the 15th century.

Arbroath Abbey (B49), now ruined, was dedicated to St Thomas à Becket. In the South Transept is a circular window known as the 'O' of Arbroath, which used to be lit up and acted as a beacon for passing ships. In 1951, the Stone of Destiny (or Scone), having been removed from Westminster Abbey, found a temporary resting place in Arbroath before being returned to England. It is now back in Scotland and kept in Edinburgh Castle along with the Honours of Scotland.

Queen Mary continued through Dundee (B45), Perth (B44), Stirling (B25) and Linlithgow (B18) and thence back to Edinburgh. She had experienced an eventful tour and seen at first hand the ruthlessness of some of her lords and the times in which she was living. For the moment, however, she would be able to enjoy the light-hearted lifestyle of the court she had established for herself, still very much run on French lines. But the turbulent years had begun.

CHAPTER 6

Henry Stuart, Lord Darnley

MARY QUEEN OF SCOTS was fully aware that in order to continue the Stuart dynasty, she would have to marry again. After the death of her first husband, King Francis II, she had become a much sought-after prize by many suitors within Scotland, England and countries on the Continent. She could afford to be choosy and take her time. After all, she was still in her early twenties.

It was not only the Queen who was turning her thoughts towards marriage but also some of those around her. James Stewart, Earl of Moray, had taken Lady Agnes Keith as his wife and three of her Four Maries were considering husbands.

Queen Mary thought that she should marry Don Carlos, son of Philip II, heir to the throne of Spain, which would strengthen Scottish links with that country. This idea was frowned upon by her uncle, the Cardinal of Lorraine, who was anxious that Spain did not become more powerful than it already was by closer links

Palace of Holyroodhouse

57

with Scotland. His preference was for Charles, the Archduke of Austria. Neither would Catherine de Medici have approved of Don Carlos, as her own daughter, Elisabeth, was married to his father and she would not wish Mary at the same court.

Fate began to take a hand. A young poet, Pierre de Châtelard, who had travelled from France, became captivated by Mary Stuart. After a masque at Holyroodhouse in which both he and the Queen had taken part, de Châtelard hid in her bedroom in the hope of making advances towards her. The plan was thwarted when he was discovered by Mary's maidservants as they were preparing their Queen for bed. De Châtelard was severely reprimanded and ordered to leave court. He undertook to return to France forthwith but, instead, was so besotted with the Queen that he continued to pursue her.

Early in 1563, Mary set out on another royal progress to Fife. She travelled to Stirling and made a short stay at Castle Campbell (B39), a forbidding fortress in the Ochil Hills, sometimes known as Castle Gloom. Mary went there to attend the wedding celebrations of the Earl of Argyll's sister to another James Stewart, Lord Doune.

Castle Campbell is set high in a wooded glen in the Ochil Hills above the little town of Dollar. It has a 15th-century square tower with 16th-century extensions. John Knox preached at the castle in 1556 and there is a large rock near a ruined archway known as John Knox's Pulpit. The road winds steeply to the car park and the visitor must walk the remainder of the way to the castle. It is well worth the effort for it is a romantic but eerie place to explore, and offers extensive views across parts of Fife and the River Forth.

The royal progress continued to Rossend Castle (B29), which overlooks the Firth of Forth. The building has been fully restored over recent years and has become the offices of a firm of architects. At Rossend de Châtelard defied the warning he had been given earlier at Holyroodhouse and again approached the Queen. He claimed he had come to bid farewell to Mary before his departure for France. This time, he forced his way into the Queen's bedroom whilst she was in a state of undress and, even though her attendants were present, attempted to molest her. Her cries for help were quickly answered by Moray, and the poet was arrested and locked in the castle dungeon. Moray had allegedly bribed a French servant, Choisseul, to watch de Châtelard. Mary stated that she had expected Moray to slay de Châtelard on the spot. However, Moray preferred to achieve the maximum amount of publicity from the incident and insisted on a public trial. Next day, the court moved on to St Andrews (B32) where de Châtelard was tried and executed in the market place on 22 February 1563. Against her will, Mary Stuart was forced by Moray to witness another execution.

On each of her royal progresses, Mary had strong support from her entourage. This usually included James Stewart, Lord Moray, her Secretary of State, Maitland, the four Maries, an apothecary, a nurse, courtiers, servants and soldiers to guard the Queen. It meant that situations such as the de Châtelard affair or other minor outbursts could swiftly be handled.

About this time the Queen received news from France that her uncle, the 2nd Duke of Guise, had been murdered by a Huguenot in the château at Blois.

From St Andrews, the court moved to Loch Leven Castle (B38) on its island setting close to Kinross, which was later to become a place of imprisonment for Queen Mary. The castle was first used as a state prison by Robert the Bruce in 1316 and passed to the Douglas family in 1390. The property was inherited around 1540 and considerably improved by Sir Robert Douglas and his wife, the former Lady Margaret Erskine. Prior to her marriage, Margaret Erskine had been a mistress of James V and was the mother of James Stewart, Mary's half-brother.

At Loch Leven the Queen held another interview with John Knox. If things looked brighter at court, religious matters were still in turmoil and taking a turn for the worse. Knox had been told of the de Châtelard affair and declared that his execution was his retribution for 'dancing'. It had been suggested that the whole affair was a Machiavellian plot by Mary's enemies in France in a bid to discredit her and thwart the current marriage negotiations. Knox had also heard rumours of Mary's intention to marry Don Carlos of Spain. He had no wish to see Scotland involved with another strong Catholic country. This resulted in another confrontation between the Queen and the head of the Reformed Church, resulting in Mary's dismissal of Knox. He persistently taunted her about her way of religion and vigorously condemned the practice of celebrating Catholic Mass.

During the summer of 1563 Mary set out on her travels once again. This time she went westwards, visiting Glasgow Castle (B24), owned by the Earl of Lennox, and Hamilton Castle, home of James Hamilton, Duke of Châtelherault. The court was bound for Dumbarton Castle (C2) where Mary had left Scotland for France as a five-year-old.

Dumbarton had been the capital of the ancient kingdom of Strathclyde – a name which was revived at the time of local government reform in 1974. It had once extended from the River Clyde as far south as Lancashire. The castle stands in a commanding position on a high volcanic rock. A 12th-century gateway and a sundial, a gift of Mary Queen of Scots, have been preserved. There is an exhibition in the Governor's House of the history of the site and its connections with Queen Mary.

From Dumbarton, Mary travelled by boat down the River Clyde and into Loch Fyne to visit one of her cousins, the Protestant Earl of Argyll, at his castle in Inveraray (C3). This pleasant little Royal Burgh stands in a richly wooded setting, surrounded by beautiful hills with a backdrop of mountains. The original castle, which Mary would have visited, was a fortified keep. In 1741, there was a complete transformation of Inveraray when the old town and castle were demolished. A new town was built half a mile away, and on the old site a palatial new residence in a landscaped setting was constructed between 1741 and 1785. This is the present Inveraray Castle, the home of the Duke of Argyll, Chief of the Clan Campbell. Inveraray Jail is a popular tourist attraction where life in a 19th-century prison is vividly depicted by uniformed prisoners and warders.

After a brief stay at Inveraray, Mary travelled south to Dunoon (C4) and Toward Castle (C5). Only a few traces of Dunoon Castle remain. Toward Castle is a ruined 15th-century tower house with an early 17th-century courtyard, gateway and ancillary buildings. It was the principal seat of the Lamonts and, in 1646, the setting of one of the ugliest incidents of the Civil War, when the entire garrison, including children, was massacred. It was probably never reoccupied after that.

From Toward, the Queen crossed the Firth of Clyde and continued on dry land. The first night in Ayrshire was spent at Lord Sempill's castle at Southannan, of which only a few stones now remain. Her host was an elderly Roman Catholic whose illegitimate son, John, later married Mary Livingston, one of the Queen's four Maries. The next night was spent at the almost-vanished Eglington Castle (C6) where Mary was guest of the Earl of Eglington, one of the nobles who had escorted her on her return from France. The expedition continued as the royal party passed south through Irvine, via Seagate Castle, and reached Ayr (C7) in time for supper. In Ayr, they were probably accommodated for two nights in the Sheriff's lodging or a private house. Ayr's most famous son is Scotland's national poet, Robert Burns, born at nearby Alloway on 25 January 1759.

From Ayr, it was only a short trip across the River Doon by the high single-arched bridge to Dunure Castle (C8) in its cliff-top setting with views to the mountain peaks of the Isle of Arran and the outline of the Kintyre peninsula. Dunure Castle was owned by the Earl of Cassillis, another Roman Catholic, who introduced the Queen to some of his relatives and other important guests.

The journey was then by way of Ardmillan (C9), the home of Thomas Kennedy, south of Girvan. Just a few ruins remain of this once-great house, tucked under a steep hill facing the sea just beyond the mouth of the Water of Girvan. They next reached Ardstinchar (C10), a spacious and lofty castle. This was the home of Kennedy of Bargany and Mary spent the night there. It was located high above the village of Ballantrae and dominated the River Stinchar. Only a single wall now remains. Leaving the Ayrshire coastline, the entourage made for the Abbey of Glenluce (C11) in Galloway. The ruined Abbey is a short way from the village up the Water of Luce. It was founded in 1192 by Roland, Lord of Galloway, for the Cistercian Order of monks. Robert the Bruce and James IV had been earlier visitors.

A well-known place of religious pilgrimage was next on the itinerary. This was Whithorn Priory (C12) in Wigtownshire, close to the Galloway coast. It has been described as 'the cradle of Christianity in Scotland' and had, for centuries, been visited by Stewart monarchs, including James V. The ruins stand on the site of an earlier church dedicated to St Ninian. It is thought to have been the very first church in Scotland. The Candida Casa of St Ninian had been founded in 397 AD, 166 years before St Columba arrived in Iona. The approach is by a 17th-century archway known as The Pend which has a panel with the Royal Arms of Scotland before the Union with England. There is little now left of this once-great Christian shrine which has maintained a strong tradition as a place of pilgrimage.

From Whithorn, the party headed north through Clary to the (now ruined) Kenmure Castle (C13) on the outskirts of New Galloway for a two-day visit with Sir John Lochinver. The castle stands at the northern end of Loch Ken. They then headed southwards again to stay with one of Mary Stuart's staunchest Catholic supporters, Hugh Montgomery, Lord Eglington, at his house at St Mary's Isle (C14), overlooking the Solway Firth. The royal party journeyed along the coast to Kirkcudbright (C15) where another priory once stood, dedicated to St Maria de Trahil. Kirkcudbright is a picturesque small town which is popular with artists.

It was then on via Terregles Castle (C20) near Dumfries on the River Nith to head in a northerly direction, calling at Drumlanrig Castle (C22), a charming building of red sandstone owned by the Douglas family. The present Renaissance castle is built on the site of the original fortress, set in parkland and overlooked by the rolling hills of Dumfriesshire. It is the home of the Duke of Buccleuch and Queensberry and, along with the Country Park, is open during the tourist season.

Aiming for Edinburgh, the party moved on to Crawfordjohn and the now-ruined Boghall Castle, home of Lady Mary Fleming's family near Biggar, and on to Skirling Castle which was demolished a few years later in 1568. They then followed the course of the River Tweed as far as Neidpath Castle (B15) near Peebles.

Neidpath Castle is set in a fine position overlooking the swift-running river. During the 14th century, the estates were held by the Frasers and then, through marriage, the Hay family took over and held them for nearly 380 years. The Hays built Neidpath Castle in the second half of the 14th century and it has walls reputed to be 11ft thick. Over recent years, the site has regularly been used for film location work including *The Bruce*.

The next overnight stay was at the double-towered Borthwick Castle (B4), a few kilometres south of Edinburgh. It dates from 1430. Borthwick was to feature in Mary's escape after her marriage to the Earl of Bothwell.

Nearing Edinburgh, they stayed at the 14th-century Rosslyn Castle (B16), overlooking the North Esk river. Nearby is Rosslyn Chapel, with its profusion of rich and elaborate carvings, notably the Prentice Pillar. This pillar is said to have been carved by an apprentice mason during his master's absence in Italy. On his return, the master killed his pupil in a fit of jealousy at his skills as a craftsman.

The final leg of Mary's progress was from Rosslyn to Craigmillar Castle (B2), one of her favourite haunts. Close by is an area known as Little France where the Queen's French servants occasionally stayed. The royal party then arrived back at the Palace of Holyroodhouse after this exhaustive tour of the western and south-western regions of Queen Mary's kingdom. The Queen had been given a warm welcome along the way in the many towns and villages she had visited. Thousands of people had turned out to see her. In addition, she had also been courteously received by many of her nobles and their families, Catholic and Protestant alike. As a public relations exercise, it had been a triumph. Now she was back in Edinburgh, she had other matters to attend to.

On her return, John Knox again condemned the Queen. Word had been received that Mary and her servants had been celebrating Mass at the many places they had stayed during their extensive progress. Once more, harsh words were exchanged.

Whilst all the speculation was going on regarding a new husband for the Queen of Scots, Elizabeth had been an anxious onlooker. She not only had the interests of England at heart but also her own well-being. The English Queen feared an alliance between Scotland and Spain. Through her ambassador, she sent a message to Mary Stuart, saying that if she would consider marriage to an Englishman, the Queen of Scots would be named as heir to the English throne. But who was available? Elizabeth wanted someone for Mary whom she could trust – perhaps even manipulate. Ideally, she preferred some-one who was unlikely to pose a threat to her own position. She had two possibilities in mind. Firstly, there was her own favourite, Robert Dudley, whom she later created Earl of Leicester.

Negotiations took place over many months regarding the sec-onding of Dudley to the Scottish court. However, it was a well-known fact that his reputation was already tarnished. His wife, Amy Robsart, had fallen down a flight of stairs and died in very suspicious circumstances. Was it an accident or had she been pushed by Dudley? Whatever the truth, he was implicated in her death but his guilt was never fully proven. The theory was that he wanted rid of his wife so he could advance his own pretensions with Elizabeth – perhaps even marry her. Once the facts were known, Elizabeth kept him at arm's length. She could never be seen to align herself with a suspected murderer. But, as an alternative, she could offer him in marriage to the Queen of Scots. Despite exten-sive negotiations, the plan came to naught.

Meanwhile, negotiations with Philip II of Spain were also failing as Don Carlos was reported to be in poor health and mentally deranged, quite unsuitable for marriage with any queen. This not only pleased Elizabeth but also John Knox and his followers in Scotland. It considerably diminished the possibility of religious and political influence on Scotland by such a strong Catholic country as Spain.

In July 1564 Queen Mary set out on another extensive progress. This time she headed northwards, via Linlithgow, with a short call at Callendar House (B19) near Falkirk, the family home of Mary Livingston. At this site are some well-preserved sections of the Antonine or Roman wall. Queen Mary was a visitor several times at the mansion during her travels between 1562 and 1567. Today's mansion is quite different in appearance from the building which Mary would have known, for it was rebuilt in the style of a French château. It is now a heritage centre covering the 600 years of the site's history.

From Callendar House, the Queen's route was via Stirling (B25), Perth (B44) and Innerpeffray Abbey (B42), originally a collegiate church dating from 1508 and used as a burial place by the Drummond clan. A visit was then made to Ruthven Castle (B43) before moving on to the richly wooded valley of the River Tay. Huntingtower, as Ruthven Castle is known today, was the home of the Ruthven family. It also has associations with James IV and with the so-called Ruthven Raid in 1582 when the Earl of Gowrie, head of the house of Ruthven, kidnapped King James VI. The restored 15th-century buildings include two towers joined at a lower level, the space between the towers being known as the Maiden's Leap. The paintings on the ceilings of Huntingtower are exquisite.

The royal party followed the banks of the meandering River Tay to Dunkeld (B46) with its ancient cathedral. Even as early as 570 AD, Celtic missionaries, known as Culdees, built a white wattle monastery there which was rebuilt in stone in 848 AD by Kenneth McAlpine. Some of the original red stones may be seen in the east gable of the choir. The cathedral dates from the 12th century.

The Queen and her entourage next moved to Blair Castle (B47), the ancient stronghold and family home of the Earls and

Dukes of Atholl close to Blair Atholl. The brilliant white baronial Castle, situated in an estate of 135 acres, is the home of the Atholl Highlanders, the only surviving private army in Europe, and officially recognised by Queen Victoria in 1844. In the Stewart Room of Blair Castle are two double portraits, one of Mary Stuart and her son James VI and the other of her parents, James V and Mary of Guise. On her visit to Blair, Mary took part in a hunt at which five wolves and 360 red deer were reported killed.

Continuing on their journey northwards, the party headed for Inverness. This time there was no resistance to Mary entering the castle after her confrontation with the Earl of Huntly's son on her previous visit. They then followed the southern bank of the Beauly Firth, and passed Beauly Priory (B61), originally built in the 13th century by monks of the Valliscaulin Order. It is thought that Beauly was so named after a comment made by the Queen of Scots during her visit – 'Beau lieu!'. Today, only the ruined church survives. The most northerly point that Mary ever travelled to was Dingwall (B62) where only slight remains are left of the castle at the foot of Castle Street.

Turning back south, she retraced her steps to Inverness and crossing the Grampians to Aberdeen, went by Dunottar Castle, Dundee and St Andrews to her favourite hunting ground in Fife. At North Queensferry, the party finally crossed the Forth for the return journey to Holyroodhouse.

Whilst Mary Stuart had been on her travels, Elizabeth had not been idle. After the Earl of Leicester had been turned down as a possible husband for her Scottish cousin, she needed someone else for the role. Though she did have reservations about his being brought up as a Catholic, there was Henry Stuart, Lord Darnley, the son of the Earl and Countess of Lennox. Darnley's mother, the former Lady Margaret Douglas, was the daughter of Margaret Tudor, sister of Henry VIII and, after Mary, could well be named as the next in line of succession to the English throne. Darnley's father, Matthew, Earl of Lennox, was also of royal blood. He had been banished from Scotland a few years earlier for taking sides father, Matthew, Earl of Lennox, was also of royal blood. He had been banished from Scotland a few years earlier for taking sides with Henry VIII against Châtelherault, the Scottish Regent at the time. Lennox had attempted to storm Dumbarton Castle (C2) in 1544 with English troops. He then moved to England where he and his wife raised two sons, Henry, Lord Darnley, and Charles Stuart. Darnley was born on 7 December 1545 at Temple Newsam House (E10), an Elizabethan mansion near Leeds in Yorkshire. Both Henry and Charles were to feature in Mary's life in future years. They came from the royal houses of Tudor and Stuart and their pedigree was impeccable.

Temple Newsam House is directly associated with the manor of Newsam in the Domesday Book of 1086 when it belonged to two Anglo-Saxon thanes, Dunstan and Glunier. The manor was then granted to Ilbert de Lacy. During the political turmoil of Edward II's reign, it was held by Robert de Holland and reverted to the crown in 1323. In 1544, Henry VIII gave the property to the Earl of Lennox, husband of his niece, Margaret. The present house was built during the Tudor period and has been added to over the centuries.

Lady Margaret, on behalf of her husband, Matthew, pleaded with Elizabeth for him to be allowed to leave England. He wanted to appeal to the Scottish court that the Lennox estates in Western Scotland, which had been confiscated, be restored to him. After some deliberation, the English Queen decided to allow him to visit Scotland in an effort to negotiate the appeal.

Around that time the name of Lennox's son, Henry Stuart, Lord Darnley, was first advanced to Mary Stuart as a possible bridegroom. (His name had also originally been spelt Stewart but he had changed it to Stuart after education in France.) Initially, there appeared to be a strong case for such a marriage. Mary and Darnley were not only first cousins but both had been brought up in the Roman Catholic faith.

Word was received from Queen Elizabeth through her ambassador, Lord Melville, that she did not consider Lord Darnley a worthy enough suitor for Mary. At the same time, she gave him permission to travel to the Scottish court on the pretext of his paying homage to her royal cousin, Queen Mary. Although Darnley was a Catholic, Elizabeth knew he had Protestant leanings, and that this could help her own cause, which was to turn Scotland into a Protestant country. Mary was not shrewd enough to realise that Elizabeth was scheming.

The Queen of Scots began yet another progress, this time to Fife, during January 1565. She headed for Falkland Palace and travelled via the now-ruined Collairnie Castle (B35) near Cupar. The next place she called at was Balmerino Abbey (B34), a Cistercian abbey founded in 1229.

Balmerino Abbey was built by monks from Melrose Abbey (E3) and stands in a delightful setting on the south shore of the Firth of Tay. The beautiful Chapter House dates from the 15th century. It was to this Abbey that James V brought his first wife, Princess Madeleine, the daughter of Francis I of France. She was a sickly girl of sixteen and only lived for a matter of weeks after her short stay.

After a few days in St Andrews, the royal party moved on to Lundin Tower (B31), near Lower Largo. In 1676, Alexander Selkirk, the prototype of Daniel Defoe's *Robinson Crusoe*, was born in Lower Largo and a statue to him stands near the harbour. Finally, the royal party moved to Wemyss Castle (B30), which dates from 1421, where Mary Stuart was to receive an unexpected visitor.

Lord Darnley appeared on 17 February 1564 at Wemyss Castle and Mary was very taken with him. He was a young, virile nineteen-year-old – tall, handsome and debonair. She soon fell for his good looks and what then appeared to be a charming personality. After all, she had up to that time probably been starved of any real love and marital affection. It is highly unlikely that her marriage to Francis had ever been consummated and she craved someone to love her for herself and not just her position. On his part, Darnley set out to impress the Queen of Scots and win her hand. After all, to achieve such a prize would be as good as securing the Kingship of Scotland – for that was his ultimate ambition.

Darnley left Wemyss to visit his father, the Earl of Lennox, who was then in Dunkeld. Mary carried on with her progress to Dunfermline Abbey (B27).

Dunfermline Abbey is an ancient shrine and the burial place of Robert the Bruce. It was founded by Queen Margaret, wife of Malcolm III, in the 11th century and was regularly used as a residence by Scottish monarchs. The abbey church has a magnificent Norman nave dating from 1150. There are no fewer than fifteen royal graves at Dunfermline which was also the birthplace of James I in 1394. The Palace and former monastic buildings were rebuilt by James VI for his Queen, Anne of Denmark, and it was here that she gave birth to the future Charles I in 1600. Something still remains of the Royal Palace, which was built out of the former monastery, notably a 200-foot long buttressed wall, and also Malcolm's Tower. The Pends archway links the Palace with the Abbey. Close by is the beautifully restored Abbot House, once part of the monastery. It is an excellent place to discover more of this historic town and its part in Scotland's history.

Within a few days, delighted with the welcome he had received from Mary, Darnley re-joined the Queen's party to cross the Forth en route to South Queensferry on their return journey to Edinburgh.

James Stewart, Earl of Moray, was against the match between Mary and Darnley from the start. During most of the time when Mary ruled Scotland by herself, James had been her closest adviser and confidant. He was the leading nobleman in Scotland. He disliked Darnley, who was four years younger than Mary. In his eyes, such a marriage could only strengthen Mary's position. As the eldest of James V's illegitimate children, James had always felt frustrated that he was not the rightful heir to the Scottish throne and he resented that Mary was Queen. Both he and Maitland, the Queen's Secretary of State, jointly wanted to maintain their power and influence over the Queen in order to rule Scotland themselves. They suspected that James Hepburn, 4th Earl of Bothwell, had similar ambitions to seize power when the opportunity arose.

Bothwell was a nobleman from the Border country who, at the time, had powerful allies. His education had been conducted by the Bishop of Moray and he was well travelled. For some time, he had had an affair with a Norwegian lady, Anna Throndsen, and it was in connection with seeking funds to support himself that he first met Mary Stuart at the court of France. He had earlier acted as Lieutenant of the Border for Mary of Guise during her Regency in the late 1550s but had been replaced by the Earl of Moray. Mary had later banished him from court on the advice of James Stewart and Maitland after a feud with the Earl of Arran's son. However, Bothwell's absence was temporary. As another of Mary's half-brothers, John Stewart, was to marry Bothwell's sister, Lady Janet Hepburn, she agreed to attend the wedding at Crichton Castle (B6), one of the family residences. John Stewart was her favourite half-brother and he had been made Commendator of Coldingham Priory (B12) by his natural father, James V. Queen Mary met Bothwell once again at the wedding.

Crichton Castle stands in an imposing, though somewhat remote, position a few kilometres south of Edinburgh, close to the source of the River Tyne. It has a curious Italianate north wing with numerous projecting bosses in the courtyard walls. The site is associated with the novel *Marmion* by Sir Walter Scott.

Mary saw no fault in Darnley, and despite the warnings of James Stewart and others around her, was completely oblivious to his misdemeanours and attitudes. In truth, he was vain, effeminate, arrogant and selfish, given to fits of temper and periods of moodiness. Yet the Queen showered presents and titles on her new lover. Once at court, Darnley formed a friendship with David Rizzio, Mary's musician, and together they fawned on the Queen of Scots. It was at this point that Queen Elizabeth issued an ultimatum that unless Mary married Robert Dudley, Earl of Leicester, she would no longer be prepared to grant her recognition as heir to the throne of England. At last it dawned on the Queen of Scots that she was being used as a pawn in one of Elizabeth's games. She decided that she would no longer listen to or take advice from her

English cousin. Mary Stuart knew who she wanted as her new husband. Her mind was already made up.

Darnley soon became a permanent member of the Queen's court and got on well at first with other courtiers. Together with Rizzio, he helped entertain the Queen by playing cards, listening to music and hunting. However, Darnley's arrogance and immaturity soon made him many enemies, especially amongst the lords, many of whom felt rejected by their Queen in the presence of her suitor. Even her four Maries could not agree with her choice. Yet Mary persisted in training her lover to play the part of Consort. The advice given her by many people was ignored. A few weeks after they had returned from the last progress, Darnley took to his bed with an illness at Stirling Castle (B25) where the court happened to be at the time. Despite criticism from her courtiers, Mary insisted on helping in person to nurse him back to good health.

Once he recovered, the Queen announced she was to bestow the title of Earl of Ross upon Darnley. To most of her Scottish nobles, both the Lords of the Congregation and Catholics alike, this appeared to be an act of defiance. It was as good as making a declaration of her intended marriage.

Mary made contact with Philip II of Spain and her uncle, the Cardinal of Lorraine, to seek their approval. Through the Cardinal, she also needed to obtain papal blessing on the marriage in view of the fact that she and Darnley were first cousins. This dispensation did not arrive until long after the marriage ceremony had taken place.

On Sunday, 29 July 1565 at six o'clock in the morning, Mary Queen of Scots, dressed in black in mourning for her first husband, Francis, was married to Henry Stuart, Lord Darnley. In contrast to Mary, Darnley wore an elaborate bejewelled outfit. Only Mary celebrated Nuptial Mass after the service. The ceremony took place in the Chapel Royal at the Palace of Holyroodhouse. Darnley was persuaded to further celebrate his marriage in the Protestant Kirk of St Giles. Within days, Mary proclaimed her new husband as King of Scots, a title for which he had been clamouring. This act was unconstitutional and it angered many of the Scottish lords as it had not been approved by the Privy Council. All was not well in other parts of Scotland. Many people were angered by the marriage. Mary Stuart, as so often during her lifetime, had been ruled by her heart rather than her head. It was to be a recipe for disaster.

CHAPTER 7

David Rizzio

THE SCOTTISH NOBLES WERE furious when they heard that Mary Stuart had made her husband King. The title, Duke of Albany, had also been bestowed on him. The Lords of the Congregation had not been consulted over either matter, and in any case, many of them disapproved of Mary's choice of husband and his behaviour since he had arrived in Scotland. They refused to recognise Darnley as having equal status with their Queen.

At the end of 1564, Mary's personal secretary, Peter Raullet, died. She gave the post to her musician, David Rizzio. This was a cause of great concern for the nobles, many of whom felt displaced by the Italian musician. What did he know about Scotland's affairs of state or foreign policy?

The combination of Mary Stuart's actions was to lead to tragic consequences for both Rizzio and Darnley and, eventually, a fall from grace by the Queen herself.

The Earl of Bothwell, at this stage, was living abroad, and he now begged Mary to let him return to Scotland. The request was granted but it displeased the Earl of Moray, who wanted rid of him for fear of any influence he might exert over the Queen. At the

Rizzio's Guitar

time, Mary was never more confident and pleased with herself at what she had achieved in her choice of husband. Who was Moray to oppose her now? Bothwell also had a set-back mainly as a result of a slanderous remark he was reputed to have made about Mary when she was in France. He alleged that she had conducted an affair with her uncle, the Cardinal of Lorraine. This angered the Queen and, at first, she had refused to allow Bothwell to return.

After the wedding ceremony at Holyroodhouse, the festivities lasted for four days. These were interrupted by a rebellion by Moray in defiance at Mary's actions, which meant that the Queen's troops had to challenge her half-brother. There was more trouble to come from this direction.

Mary wished to show off her new husband, the King Consort, to her subjects and they set off on yet another royal progress. She took with her her usual entourage which included David Rizzio, now in the role of Secretary. They left on 26 August for Stirling, then went on to Perth, Innerpeffray Abbey, Ruthven Castle, Dunkeld and back to Edinburgh via Callandar House.

The relationship between Darnley and Moray quickly deteriorated. Soon Moray was making the claim to Mary that her new husband was after his blood. News reached the Queen's ears that Moray was planning to abduct both Darnley and his father, the Earl of Lennox, and take them back to England. At this the Queen demanded to see her half-brother. He refused to meet her to discuss the matter and was branded a traitor.

At this stage, the Protestant Lords had no wish to see the illegitimate Moray replace his sister. A number of them rallied to her call to arms and Bothwell was also recalled to Edinburgh in the hope he might fight on the side of the Queen. He had a reputation as a reckless but brave warrior and Darnley soon grew to resent the tough Borderer who had been put in charge of Mary's army. Darnley had already chosen his own father to lead their troops into battle. The new King got his way.

Moray and his followers made an effort to obtain more military assistance in Edinburgh but were shadowed by Queen Mary and her troops. Their quest to follow Moray and defeat him led westwards through Linlithgow and Stirling to Glasgow and Kilsyth. It then took them into Fife, to Dunfermline Abbey, Loch Leven

Castle, Falkland Palace and St Andrews, then to Dundee (B45) and Ruthven Castle. They rode on to Perth and back to Dunfermline before making the return journey to Edinburgh. The military operation took the Queen and her troops back to Linlithgow and Stirling and then as far as Dumfries in the south-west, in an attempt to capture Moray before he could escape to England.

Mary had pursued the rebels from place to place, sometimes doubling back in order to discover their whereabouts. They were thin on the ground with regard to strength of numbers and hoped for Elizabeth's assistance with soldiers and arms. They waited in vain. While Mary was journeying to the west, the rebels arrived in Edinburgh to try and rally more support for their cause, but found there were few who would come to their aid. Even the cannons at Edinburgh Castle were pointed at them. They miscalculated the people's attitude and discovered that Mary had the support of the townsfolk of Edinburgh and most of her other subjects.

Moray, in an effort to gather English support for his cause which was to seize Mary's throne, managed to reach the border with England. All Elizabeth offered to do was negotiate with Mary to allow him to return to Scotland. After Elizabeth's apparent dismissal, there was nothing left for Moray than to accept defeat. The whole ill-fated affair became known as the Chaseabout Raid.

One pleasant little interlude Mary and Darnley experienced before their return to Edinburgh was their stay at Lochmaben Castle (C21) in Annandale, Dumfriesshire. They attended a banquet which was probably held to celebrate the fact that Moray and his rebel lords had just fled to Carlisle. The 13th-century Lochmaben Castle was once the seat of Robert the Bruce's family. It became a favourite residence of James IV. James V also used the castle and went there on 22 November 1542 before his proposed invasion of England. His army was routed two days later at the Battle of Solway Moss (C24).

Bothwell was now anxious to further his ambitions by marrying into an illustrious family. A marriage was therefore negotiated with Lady Jean Gordon, sister to the new Earl of Huntly, despite her protestations. The marriage took place at the Canongate Kirk (A7) in Edinburgh, and the chief guest at the wedding was Mary Queen of Scots. The new King was also present.

Darnley's behaviour began to worsen towards all those around him. His vanity, bad temper and insolence became intolerable. He demanded of Mary that he be granted the Crown Matrimonial which would set him on equal footing with his wife. This Mary always refused. The storm clouds started to gather as their relationship began to deteriorate.

The Lords of the Congregation and John Knox were angered by the behaviour of Darnley and the thought of what might happen if he were given equal status. It could mean that if the Queen died, Darnley would reign as a puppet King manipulated by Queen Elizabeth. It soon became known that he was consorting with prostitutes and other persons of disrepute. News of his evening 'expeditions' got back to Mary who, at first, turned a blind eye, but as she began to realise just how bad his behaviour had become, she grew suspicious of his actions and motives.

More and more she relied upon her Secretary, David Rizzio, in whom she confided over many matters of state and religious policy. This would often be without any consultation with Darnley, and he resented strongly the little musician who had risen to such an important position at the Scottish court. Not unnaturally, the nobles also disapproved of Rizzio's influence. Jealousies started to creep in. Darnley and the Lords realised that at last they had something in common.

Despite his aspirations and demands for the Crown Matrimonial, Darnley was completely lacking with regard to his responsibilities towards the State. He soon became bored with officialdom and much preferred to go hunting or seek out other sports and interests. Often he indulged in bouts of drunkenness and had to be helped back to Holyroodhouse. This caused much displeasure and disagreement between him and Mary as all official papers had to be counter-signed by both of them. On many occasions when this was needed, Darnley was not at court. The only way that Mary could save herself from embarrassment was to obtain a stamp of his signature which could be used in his absence. He was rarely available for audiences and other functions involving foreign ambassadors, ministers and important guests. He completely neglected his duties as King and Consort.

After the Chaseabout Raid and the turmoil brought about by Moray in his opposition to Mary's choice of husband, rumours were circulating that the Queen had contacted Philip II of Spain for assistance against the outlawed Protestant nobles. This began to undermine the confidence of her subjects and Mary needed to re-establish her support of the Reformed religion. She suggested to Darnley that he might be seen to attend services at the Kirk of St Giles to confirm the royal couple's support for John Knox and his followers. This proved to be disastrous, as Knox used the opportunity to condemn Catholic rites and the behaviour of the Queen's court at Holyroodhouse. His sermon was preached on the text 'O, Lord our God, other lords than Thou have ruled over us'. The preacher illustrated his text with other quotations and references to Scotland, dwelling on the unsatisfactory situation of a kingdom being governed by women and boys. Darnley took the remarks as personal criticism and stormed out of the church. The new King had become a liability. How much longer could Mary trust him?

Knox was called from his bed to appear before the Privy Council, where he was informed by Lethington that he had been suspended from preaching whilst the King and Queen were in Edinburgh. A week later, Mary and Darnley left Edinburgh. Knox immediately resumed his radical preaching against the Crown.

In November of that year Mary became ill, complaining of a pain in her side. She went to Linlithgow Palace to convalesce and it was discovered that she was nearly three months pregnant. The thought of an heir was a great boost to her morale as she realised it would strengthen her hand in her claim for the English throne for herself and her successors.

Mary had become more dependant on Rizzio as her marriage to Darnley deteriorated. When Darnley learned of his wife's pregnancy, he confronted her with the allegation that Rizzio was the father and not himself. This was hardly likely to be true, as the baby had been conceived around the time of Mary's visit to Dumfries in the autumn when Darnley had accompanied her in pursuit of Moray and his fellow rebels.

On learning the news about Mary Stuart's pregnancy, Queen Elizabeth was angered and frustrated that her royal cousin was with child whilst she herself remained unmarried. Officially, she sent greetings via the English ambassador to Mary for her well-being. Never having met Mary in person, Elizabeth persistently asked questions about her appearance, the colour of her hair, her musical accomplishments and her pastimes. The English Queen had no intention of feeling inferior to her great rival north of the border. The gap and animosity between them was to widen with the years.

CHAPTER 8

Murder Most Foul

DAVID RIZZIO WAS NOT attractive in the physical sense. He was dark-skinned and swarthy, and reputed to have a hunched back. His attributes were that he had a pleasing manner, was a good musician, shrewd and tactful, with a good ear for any news from the Continent, especially France or Spain. Some thought he was in the pay of the Pope but that is unlikely. He had a good network of contacts who fed information to him through gossip from foreign ambassadors, priests and other Roman Catholic supporters. This infiltration of the Scottish court by someone who was not a Scot was frowned upon. Yet the Queen trusted him implicitly.

Though not as blatant as Darnley, Rizzio enjoyed his power over those at court, especially those nobles who craved an audience with Queen Mary. As a member of Mary's inner sanctum he had access to the Queen at all reasonable times. He insisted that all matters for the Queen should first pass through his hands for initial vetting and approval. In short, he was becoming over-pompous. He was not averse to a little bribery if any particular Lord was seeking a favour from the Queen. This sort of thing became irksome to those who had to deal with him.

Due to Darnley's increasing absence from her social life as well as the time she spent on state business, Mary became completely dependant on Rizzio. He was always near at hand to advise or comfort her when she was faced with any difficult situations or decisions.

As her pregnancy progressed, Mary spent more time on leisure pursuits and, as circumstances would allow, less on state affairs. Her popularity was slowly starting to erode, especially with those Lords of the Congregation who were still living in exile in England. They were particularly angered by her intention to have their lands and buildings confiscated through the Scottish Parliament and they wanted to return home. Other nobles such as Maitland and Morton resented the Queen's confidences with Rizzio. Added to this was the continuing onslaught by John Knox and members of his Presbyterian church. All together, opposition to Mary Stuart was beginning to get very serious.

Darnley and the Lords of the Congregation began to use Rizzio as a whipping boy, blaming him when matters went awry or did not meet with their approval. The King poured scorn on the little Italian and used him to get back at Mary in his jealousy.

Matters were coming to a head when Moray suggested that Darnley be crowned King and granted the Crown Matrimonial. The flames of trouble were also fanned by the constant suggestions to Darnley that the Queen had been having an affair with her Secretary. Naturally, the King was happy to believe what he was told but still persisted in his life of debauchery and misconduct.

Despite her confinement, the Queen insisted that the Scottish Parliament meet in March to confirm the confiscation of lands and properties of Moray and the rebels who had supported him in the rebellion against the Crown. None were pardoned except Châtelherault on condition that he stayed away from Scotland for a further five years.

In view of the edict, the Moray proposals for Darnley to obtain the Crown Matrimonial and the Protestant Lords to be restored became major issues amongst those who would benefit from such action. A secret document was produced by all dissenters to the Parliamentary decisions who were still based in Scotland. Moray was in Newcastle and therefore close enough to receive news fairly swiftly. Although absent from Scotland, he put his name to the declaration along with his fellow rebels. In particular, they made sure that the signature of the King was also included as positive proof of his implication in the matter. In essence, the three-pronged document set out, officially, to work towards the granting of the Crown Matrimonial to Darnley, the pardoning and return of the Lords who had been expelled from Scotland, and the continuance of the Protestant faith. There was a further clause which really underlined the main reason for the pact though it was not actually stated. 'So shall they not spare life or limb in setting forward all that may bend to the advancement of the King's honour.' The implication of this statement was to become clearer as events started to unfold.

Another document was drawn up by the King and the Lords who were planning to get rid of Rizzio. It included words to the effect that the King would assume full responsibility for the murder of the Italian Secretary.

News of the plot reached the English court. Both Elizabeth and her Secretary, William Cecil, were aware of the plan. However, the Protestant lords were careful that Mary should not have wind of what was about to happen. Nor were Bothwell or Huntly told. By this time, Bothwell had been pardoned by the Queen and restored to his former standing as Lieutenant of the Borders. She had created Lord John Gordon, who had raised a northern force during the Chaseabout Raid, the new Earl of Huntly. Their mutual dislike of Moray, who had been the cause of Bothwell's imprisonment and the downfall of the Gordon family, drew the two men together.

Elizabeth's agent in Scotland, Thomas Randolph, wrote to Cecil that with the consent of the King, Rizzio was to have his throat cut within ten days. The only warning the victim received was from an astrologer who told him to 'Beware of the bastard'. The Italian was not unduly worried by this statement, thinking that the reference was to Moray who, at that time, was ensconced on the other side of the English border. He had forgotten about another illegitimate nobleman, George Douglas, the King's uncle.

Things appeared quite normal on the Saturday afternoon when King Henry played a game of tennis with Rizzio. By this time, Moray, fully aware of the plan, was returning from Newcastle to Edinburgh with an escort provided by the King. As dusk began to fall, Morton and a body of men surrounded Holyroodhouse whilst Bothwell and Huntly were dining with Lethington.

The Queen was having supper on the second floor of her apartments in a turret room in the north-west corner of the Palace. Her rooms consisted of a large reception room, or Outer Chamber, where she received official visitors; leading off was the Queen's Bed Chamber; and beyond were two much smaller rooms in each corner. One of these was a dressing room, the other used as a supper room. The King's suite of rooms was situated below on the first floor.

On the ceiling of the Outer Chamber are carved shields which commemorate Mary's first marriage to Francis II of France when he was Dauphin. It was in this room that Mary held her confrontational meetings with John Knox and with the various Scottish nobles and foreign ambassadors. Today in this room the visitor can see the Darnley Jewel which was originally made for Lord Darnley's mother, the Lady Margaret Douglas, Countess of Lennox, in memory of her husband and son. There are samples of Mary Stuart's embroidery completed during her long years of captivity in England. There is also a miniature portrait of Mary painted by the French painter, Clouet, and a silver pomander which reputedly was owned by the Queen. There are a number of other paintings and exhibits associated with the Tudor and Stuart dynasties.

In Mary Queen of Scots' Bed Chamber, the original timber ceiling is emblazoned with decorative embellishments, including the initials of the Queen and her son, James VI. Flemish tapestries adorn the walls, and over the fireplace is a painting of the Adoration of the Magi by Andrea Schiavone. Around the upper part of the walls is a beautiful frieze which was painted in 1617 during the reign of James VI.

Perhaps more intriguing are the two smaller rooms which are set between two staircases. The Wardrobe or Dressing Room was used by the monarch to by-pass the main route through the royal apartments. But it is the northern of these two rooms which catches the attention of most visitors, for it was here on the evening of 12 March 1566 that Mary was enjoying supper with close friends, including her half-brother, Lord Robert Stewart, Commendator of Holyroodhouse, her half-sister, Jean, Countess of Argyll, and her musician and Secretary, David Rizzio. At the time, Mary Stuart was six months pregnant.

The Queen and her guests had hardly begun their meal when a tapestry at one end of the room was lifted to reveal Darnley. He had entered via a narrow spiral staircase which led from his own apartments immediately below. He had already had his meal and appeared, for once, to be in a very good mood. This was contrary to his usual behaviour. He sat down beside Mary who was at one end of the table with Rizzio at the other. King Henry's sudden amorous approach gave rise to the thought that he was intoxicated through drink.

Suddenly, the tapestry was lifted again to reveal the sallow face of Lord Ruthven, who was rumoured to be rather sick at the time. He was dressed in full armour over his mantle. Ruthven addressed his remarks to the Queen. 'May it please your Majesty, to let yonder man Davie come forth of your presence, for he has been overlong here.' To this Mary replied, 'What offence hath he made?' Ruthven retorted 'Great offence!'

Mary then challenged Darnley, demanding to know what his part was in what appeared to amount to a conspiracy. He made no reply. Angrily the Queen ordered Ruthven to leave the room at once or be tried as a traitor. He ignored her. At this point Mary stood up and was grabbed by Darnley. Rizzio realised what was about to happen and cowered behind the Queen clutching at her skirts. He drew his dagger. Suddenly, the door leading from the main staircase was flung open and the other conspirators appeared.

In the ensuing scuffle, the Countess of Argyll managed to grab the last candle before it was snuffed out and the table knocked over. Lord Lindsay pushed a chair forward in the direction of the pregnant Queen's stomach whilst Ruthven grabbed his own dagger and brandished it in the direction of Rizzio who was then dragged, kicking and screaming, across the floor of the Queen's Bedroom Chamber by the conspirators. They forced him through the Presence Chamber to the top of the stairs as his terrified voice was heard exclaiming, 'Mercy, mercy! Save my life, Madame! Save my life!' The Queen could do nothing to help. The first knife thrust was made by George Douglas, the illegitimate brother of the Earl of Morton, as he grabbed Darnley's dagger, thus fulfilling the prediction which Rizzio had earlier been told – to 'beware of the bastard'. One after another, the Lords thrust their daggers into the little Italian – fifty-seven times in total, and his corpse was thrown onto a chest in the Outer Chamber. Later he was given a pauper's burial in Holyrood Cemetery.

After the mob of conspirators had left, seeking out Bothwell and Huntly as their next victims, Mary sent the Countess to discover what had been the fate of her favourite musician. She was heartbroken to learn that Rizzio was dead. Meanwhile, the wily Bothwell and Huntly had managed to escape from Holyroodhouse through a back window of the Palace to avoid a similar fate.

Early next morning the King entered Queen Mary's bed chamber and was calmly received. He had undoubtedly been terrified by events the previous night. Mary might have thought that Darnley had been used by the nobles as a tool to further their own ends, as indeed she had been. She persuaded him that his personal situation was now as dangerous as her own. She also thought that Rizzio's murder was to have been the start of an attack on herself and her unborn child by those who wished to see their own royal aspirations advanced or reinstated.

Mary therefore received the other conspirators calmly and stated that she was prepared to overlook recent events. Moray returned to Holyroodhouse two days later. Unaware that he had been part of the plot, Mary greeted him as a long lost brother. Despite her assurances of a pardon, the Lords were very sceptical about their Queen's true intentions. That same evening she summoned some of her closest aides who had been with her on that fateful night. She outlined her plans to escape with Darnley. At midnight, they would ride towards Dunbar (B11), a distance of forty kilometres. Horses were made ready, and at the given time Mary and Darnley and their supporters set off. They were joined by Bothwell and Huntly. They stopped at Seton House (B7), the home of Lord George Seton, cousin to Darnley. He was the father of Mary Seton and a loyal supporter of the Queen, and was to accompany her for the remainder of the journey to Dunbar.

The Seton House of Mary's day had been rebuilt from the castle that once occupied the site and was desecrated during the Rough Wooing in 1544. It had two frontages and a triangular courtyard. The State Apartments, as at Holyroodhouse, were on the upper floors. Not much of the original structure remains and the present house gives little indication of the original except for the vaulted ground floor which dates from the 16th century. In the grounds is the late-14th-century Collegiate Church of Seton (B7). It has a fine vaulted chancel and apse, and good window tracery.

Bearing in mind that Mary Stuart was heavily pregnant when she made the overnight journey to Dunbar, it must have been an arduous and uncomfortable experience. Soon after their arrival, they were joined by other lords who were rallying to her cause. Support was building and, between them, the nobles got together a total of 8,000 men.

Little remains today of Dunbar Castle which stands on a rock above the harbour. It has a long history including a siege in 1339. Over the years much of the castle has collapsed and fallen into the sea.

After four days at Dunbar, Mary was able to ride back to Edinburgh at the head of her new army with King Henry beside her. In her absence, the conspirators to Rizzio's murder had fled when they heard that the King had changed loyalties. Only Moray remained in Edinburgh with the comforting thought that he had arrived at Holyroodhouse after the murder had taken place. For the time being, he was safe.

One of the first things Mary arranged when she arrived back was to have Rizzio's body exhumed and re-buried according to Catholic rites, supposedly in the south-eastern corner of Canongate Churchyard (A7). She sent for Moray and informed him that she was willing to make a compromise with him and his supporters who had been involved in the Chaseabout Raid campaigns. However, there would be no leniency shown towards Rizzio's murderers. The conspirators were ordered to appear before the full Privy Council along with other lords, both Protestant and Catholic. Darnley was present alongside Mary. Some of Rizzio's murderers escaped. Others were condemned to death.

As Mary pondered over events of previous days, she realised that she could never trust Darnley again. But whatever her private feelings, publicly she had to be seen to support him. After all, they were still King and Queen. Even in those days, the maxim in royal circles was always 'put up and shut up'. Undoubtedly, Mary must have begun to loathe his presence although he was the father of her unborn child. He had proved himself to be weak, vain and spoiled, quite unequal to Kingship, and had been used by others in their greed.

In view of the forthcoming birth and her own safety, Mary Stuart moved from Holyroodhouse to Edinburgh Castle on 3 April 1566.

Edinburgh Castle, set high on a volcanic rock, has a long and proud history, the epitome of Scotland's heritage, going back to legendary times. Actual recorded history of the site started in the 11th century during the reign of Malcolm III. The Castle was taken by Edward I in 1296 and re-taken in 1313 by Randolph, Earl of Moray, for Robert the Bruce who defortified it. It was later taken and re-fortified by Edward III in 1337, and subsequently recaptured by the Scots in 1341. The Castle is approached from the Esplanade over the drawbridge and gatehouse, flanked by statues of King Robert the Bruce (1274-1329) on the left, and Sir William Wallace (1270-1305) on the right. Wallace fought tirelessly to free his country from constant domination by England. He died a martyr's death at the hands of Edward I in London.

The oldest building in the Castle is the restored Chapel of St Margaret, set on the pinnacle of the Castle Rock, commemorating the saintly Queen Margaret who died in 1093. It is one of Scotland's oldest ecclesiastical buildings. The Old Palace, built between the 15th and 17th centuries contains the Crown Room in which the Honours of Scotland are kept, including the ancient crown of Scottish monarchs and the recently returned Stone of Destiny (or Scone) on which most English or British monarchs have been crowned in Westminster Abbey. Queen Mary's Apartments are reached from the Palace Yard through a doorway over which are carved the motifs MS and HD 1566 (Mary Stuart and Henry Darnley). In these apartments is the room in which Mary gave birth to Prince James.

Mary must have been in constant fear of what might happen when the baby was born. Would her enemies try to steal the child, or even kill it? What would happen if she herself died at the birth? And what would be Darnley's stance? Her mind was filled with so many questions, for which she had no positive answers. Mary felt she had achieved some success when she was able to bring about a reconciliation between the Earl of Moray and Bothwell and Huntly. Darnley was not party to this. He continued his life of whoring and fornication in and about the town whenever the opportunity presented itself. Mary had drawn up a will, in case she did not survive the birth, leaving everything to the child. However, she did make certain provisions in Darnley's favour.

After a difficult birth, the baby was born on 19 June 1566. It was a healthy baby boy. Scotland had a new heir to the throne.

There were great celebrations throughout Scotland at the birth of the prince. Bonfires were lit, royal salutes were fired, and a thanksgiving service was held in the Kirk of St Giles. News was taken to Queen Elizabeth at the English court by Sir James Melville. She paused thoughtfully and then exclaimed, 'The Queen of Scots is lighter of a fair son and I am but a barren stock!' She knew that, with the birth of the child, Mary Stuart's hand was strengthened as next in line to her own throne.

Mary took the baby to Stirling Castle (B25) and gave him into the custody of Lord Erskine, whom she had earlier created the Earl of Mar. The Earls of Mar were the traditional custodians of royal children.

Whereas Mary and those around her greeted the birth with joy and great enthusiasm, King Henry showed very little feeling. He was still harbouring the thought that the child might have been David Rizzio's. The Queen swore to him that none other than he was the father. Darnley knew full well that the new baby had displaced him in the pecking order and he became sullen in the extreme.

The time that Mary and Darnley spent in each other's company grew less and less. Occasionally, they would attend state functions together, as protocol demanded. At the Earl of Mar's invitation, Mary travelled in July to Alloa Tower (B26), his ancestral home, for a short visit as part of her recuperation from the birth.

The history of Alloa Tower goes back to the 14th century when the Erskine family first arrived in Alloa. The tower was re-designed by the 6th Earl in the early 1700s to link it with the adjacent mansion. In 1800 there was a disastrous fire which destroyed many family heirlooms and the supposedly only authentic portrait of Queen Mary in Scotland. Alloa Tower has undergone much restoration work over recent years and was re-opened by Queen Elizabeth II in July 1997. It is possible to climb to the top of the building and enjoy spectacular views across the River Forth.

The following month the Queen and King were invited by John Stewart, Captain of the Queen's Guard, to spend some time at Traquair House (B14) near Innerleithen in the Border country, to do some hunting. Mary and Darnley ranted and raved at one another and John Stewart had to intervene.

Traquair House is one of the most romantic and oldest inhabited houses in Scotland. It has played host to no fewer than twenty-seven monarchs. Traquair was once the home of William the Lion, who held court there in 1209. The main block of the house dates from 1642 and wings were added later the same century. Of

particular interest to visitors is the bed said to have been used by
Mary Queen of Scots, her rosary and crucifix, a Royal Command
document to Sir John Stewart signed by Mary and Darnley, and a
cradle used for their son, James VI of Scotland. The main avenue
gates have not been opened since 1796 when the 7th Countess of
Traquair died. Tradition has it that they had already been closed
after 1745, not to be re-opened until a Stuart should once more
ascend the throne.

Darnley threatened he would leave Scotland for France where
he would live off some of Mary's dowries. He began a correspondence with the French and Spanish courts and the papal authorities in Rome. He condemned his wife's actions and professed that
she was not being true to her Roman Catholic religion. Despite a
meeting between the royal couple and the French ambassador, no
solution was found. Increasingly, Mary turned for support and
advice to her three closest nobles – Moray, Bothwell and Huntly.

Early in October, the Queen had to travel to Jedburgh in the
Borders on official business of the administration of justice. An
important part of the system was the holding of circuit courts – or
justice ayres – which were frequently attended by the Sovereign. In
view of continuing violence in the Border country, the Queen and
her Privy Council felt it was time to deal with the many disputes
and offences which had disturbed the area. In addition, Mary
thought that another royal progress to that part of Scotland might
help consolidate her position after the death of Rizzio. Darnley
was invited to accompany Mary but preferred to go hunting elsewhere. The entourage left Edinburgh by way of Borthwick Castle
(B4) for Melrose (E3), and rode into Jedburgh (E4) on 9 October.
Mary was accompanied by various nobles including Moray,
Huntly, Atholl, Livingston, Seton, Secretary Maitland, John Leslie,
Bishop of Ross, and other supporters.

During her time in Jedburgh, Mary is reputed to have stayed initially at a house in the High Street which is now the Spread Eagle
Hotel. Close to the town centre are the ruins of Jedburgh Abbey,
badly damaged during the Rough Wooing. The Abbey was founded

in 1138 and built of local red sandstone. It is noted for its splendid nave. The West Front includes a fine rose window known as St Catherine's Wheel. The central tower has been much restored but the 14th-century north transept is still in good condition.

The court sessions in Jedburgh had to be interrupted due to an incident which had occurred closer to the English border. The Earl of Bothwell was Keeper of Hermitage Castle (E5), a grim royal fortress in desolate countryside. In his capacity as Lieutenant of the Borders, Bothwell had been charged with bringing to justice certain notorious offenders and had set off in advance of the royal party with 300 horsemen. The feud between the Armstrongs of Liddesdale and the Johnstones of Nithsdale was his first case. Bothwell then turned his attention to the troublesome Elliots and, in a scuffle, was wounded and carried back to Hermitage Castle. The skirmish is commemorated in the Border ballad, *Little Jock Elliott*.

Hermitage Castle was once a stronghold of the Douglas clan and is surrounded by moorland overlooking the Hermitage Water in Liddesdale, a little to the west of the Newcastleton-to-Hawick road. The old hermitage, from which the castle takes its name, can still be seen a short distance upstream. The castle is a structure of immense strength, dating from 1242. The building consists of four towers and connecting walls and the interior contains the remains of the original tower.

News of Bothwell's wounding reached Mary at the beginning of her stay in Jedburgh and, contrary to popular belief, she did not rush over to Hermitage when she heard the news. At that point, no physical attraction between the two had outwardly been expressed. Two days after court business had been completed, the Queen set out with Moray and other supporters and rode over to Hermitage for consultation with Bothwell. They returned the same day, a round trip of over 80 kilometres. On route Mary lost her French-made watch, a reminder of happier days. Over 250 years later, in 1817, the watch was unearthed by a mole. The return journey was made in deteriorating weather conditions over very rough country. The Queen was thrown from her horse on a stretch of treacherous bogland, now known as The Queen's Mire. She was taken to a nearby farmhouse, not far from Hawick, in order that her clothes could be dried and repaired. Each year, this is commemorated during the July festival of Jethart Callants, when a team of horseriders from Jedburgh make the trip as far as The Queen's Mire and back again.

When the Queen's party arrived back in Jedburgh, they were exhausted, and two days later Mary Stuart became gravely ill, losing her sight and speech. She was also overcome by convulsions and vomiting. It was only four months since she had given birth and she complained frequently of a pain in her side.

She was carried in a litter to a fortified house near the centre of Jedburgh, a little to the east of the Jed Water. The house was owned by the Kerr family of nearby Ferniehirst Castle, and is now known as Mary Queen of Scots' House, one of Scotland's most popular visitor attractions. It was refurbished and re-opened in 1987 for the 400th anniversary of Queen Mary's death, and is now a museum devoted to the life and memory of the tragic Queen. There are a number of items of 'Maryana' on view including a death mask, items of jewellery and documents. One of the building's features is that it has a left-handed spiral staircase, made for the Kerrs in the 16th century. It appears that they were a left-handed family, and the staircase was so built in order that, in case of attack, they could wield their swords more easily.

As Mary Queen of Scots lay recovering in Jedburgh, James Bothwell's wounds were beginning to heal. This news gave encouragement to Mary who knew that she herself had been almost at the point of death.

When Darnley finally arrived in Jedburgh, he was given a cool reception by the nobles. He stayed for one night only in a house owned by Lord Home and then returned to Edinburgh. Bothwell had arrived in Jedburgh some days before Darnley, borne on a horse litter. He had recovered reasonably well though his face was badly scarred. The Queen's recovery was slower, but she was finally able to leave Jedburgh on 9 November. They set off for Kelso (E1) to hold a further court, and then went on to Hume Castle (B13), situated near Greenlaw in Berwickshire. This castle is now ruined and an impressive folly was built on the site in the 18th century.

Escorted by almost 1,000 horsemen, Mary viewed Berwick from a distance, exchanging courtesies with Sir John Foster, the English Governor, who rode out to meet her. The cavalcade then proceeded to Eyemouth and Coldingham Priory (B12) where Mary's half-brother, John Stewart, was Commendator.

Coldingham Priory, situated on the Berwickshire coast, dates from the 7th century. It came to prominence when the Abbey was granted to Benedictine monks in the 11th century by King Edgar. After it was extended, it became a priory and accommodated important visitors on their journeys between England and Scotland. Over many decades, it fell into disrepair until the 19th century when a new parish church was built, using stones taken from the 13th-century extensions. The parish church is still in use, but just a few ornate ruins now remain of the original priory.

The Queen's route led to Dunbar Castle (B11) once again, and then Tantallon Castle (B10) near North Berwick. Tantallon, a moated building situated on a headland facing out to the island known as the Bass Rock, dates from the 14th century. It was probably built by William Douglas, son of George, first Earl of Angus. It was twice under siege, in 1491 and 1528. The 6th Earl, Archibald, married the widow of James IV. He changed allegiance on a number of occasions. During the time of the Rough Wooing he sided with the English – perhaps to protect his own property and estates. He reverted to supporting Scotland after the desecration of family tombs in Melrose Abbey by the English. Although Cromwellian forces attacked Tantallon Castle in 1651, it withstood the siege, but over the centuries has fallen into ruin.

The royal party finally arrived back on the outskirts of Edinburgh to stay at Craigmillar Castle (B2) on 20 November.

Craigmillar Castle is a fine ruined building in a splendid elevated position with views across Edinburgh and the River Forth. It is thought to have been built by Sir Simon Preston of Gorton when he assumed the barony in 1374. His arms are over the entrance door. At the time of Mary Queen of Scots, the Castle was held by another Sir Simon Preston who was Provost of Edinburgh and a supporter of the monarchy. Most of the 17th-century lower house still stands, including the hall and a fine vaulted apartment with a large Gothic chimney breast.

The big question which Mary Queen of Scots and her lords must now consider was – what could be done about Henry Stuart, Lord Darnley, King of Scots?

The matter would soon be settled once and for all.

CHAPTER 9

James Hepburn, 4th Earl of Bothwell

THE QUESTION OF DIVORCE was at the forefront of many minds as the lords held a conference at Craigmillar Castle (B2) about the state of the royal marriage and, in particular, the outrageous behaviour of King Henry.

In those days, divorce might be granted by the papal authorities when a couple pleaded that their blood relationship was too close. Occasionally, an annulment of a marriage was granted under such conditions. However, Mary realised that if this step were taken, it could mean that, should the marriage be declared null and void, it would make her son, James, illegitimate. She knew quite well what this would mean after the continuing argument over the birth of her royal cousin, Elizabeth. This action would exclude James from the royal lineage and bring Darnley back into running as the next in line. Clearly this was not the course to take. She must therefore work towards a closer relationship with the wayward King, despite the difficulties that might lie ahead.

Unknown to the Queen, a pact was signed by some of her closest supporters – including Bothwell, Huntly, Maitland, Argyll and Moray – for the removal of Lord Darnley.

James VI's Cradle

During her stay at Craigmillar, Mary was able to recuperate. When she was feeling a little better, the court moved to Stirling Castle (B25) in preparation for the baptism of Prince James. Although the

been consulted over the question of the godparents and he sulked in another part of the castle. Queen Mary had invited Queen Elizabeth of England, Charles IX of France and the Duke of Savoy to be godparents. Each of them was represented by proxy. With great ceremony, Prince James was baptised in the Chapel Royal of Stirling Castle on 17 December 1566.

In an effort to mend her marriage, Mary, accompanied by her lords, went northwards with Darnley. The first call was at Tullibardine (B40) where the Queen celebrated her majority at the age of twenty-five. Their destination was Drummond Castle (B41) near Crieff, the home of Lord Drummond. The castle was bombarded by Cromwell in 1745. It was re-built and an old tower of the original castle remains. The site has fine terraces, gardens and topiary, all laid out in the form of the St Andrew's Cross.

Early in 1567 Darnley fell ill and decided to retreat to Glasgow (B24) where his relatives, the Lennox family, owned property and estates. His father was at Lennox Castle to take care of him. The Castle stood on the site of the present Glasgow Royal Infirmary. Darnley was rumoured to have smallpox but it is thought he could have been suffering from syphilis. His appearance changed rapidly and he took to wearing a mask to cover his pock-marked face.

The Queen returned to Holyroodhouse with her baby son. In mid-January she went to Glasgow to accompany her husband back to Edinburgh. It is alleged that in Glasgow she stayed at Provands Lordship house (B24), the oldest dwelling in the city, but this is doubtful. It has also been said that she wrote the 'Casket Letters', incriminating her in Darnley's murder, in this house. According to the Duke of Hamilton in his book, *The Crucial Years*, Mary stayed at the nearby Archbishop's Palace. Crookston Castle (B23) was another Lennox stronghold where the Queen might have been accommodated.

Crookston Castle was built by the Stewarts of Darnley in the 15th century on the site of a wooden fortress dating from around 1180 and the time of Robert Croc who gave his name to Crookston. Croc's circular defence moat is still crossed to reach the ruined castle which consists of a central tower with four square corner towers. It is situated in woodland on a hilltop which affords panoramic views across Glasgow to the Campsie Fells. With the urban sprawl which has developed over the centuries, it is perhaps hard to imagine what the rural scene would have been like in Mary's day. Instead of tower blocks of flats, the only interruptions in the landscape would have been the occasional tower houses dotted on both sides of the River Clyde.

Mary had been advised that it was unsafe for Darnley to stay in Glasgow where he might become the focus of plots against her. In Edinburgh she had sufficient protection both for herself and her son. She might well have induced the King back to Holyroodhouse with the promise of the resumption of full marital relations. However, as well as the fact that he was still suffering from his infectious illness which would put his baby son, James, and everyone else at Holyroodhouse at risk, Darnley felt it was not safe to return there after what had happened to David Rizzio. Neither did he wish to stay at Craigmillar. A compromise was reached, and a house at Kirk o' Field, a short distance from Holyroodhouse, was chosen. The house at Kirk o' Field stood on the site of the present Old College building of the University of Edinburgh.

The Queen of Scots had come to rely more and more on her closest nobles for support, in particular the Earl of Bothwell. He already had a reputation as a philanderer and his manly bearing, tough approach and rugged features would undoubtedly have been in sharp contrast to the flamboyance and prettiness of Darnley. In any case, the early love which Mary felt for Darnley had now withered. It was natural that she would be drawn towards the swarthy Borderer, as masculine as her husband was effeminate. He had earlier been the only one of her nobles who had stayed loyal to her, and had never been in the pay of either Henry VIII or Elizabeth as others had been. Mary began to take Bothwell into her confidence, and he readily reciprocated as he was ambitious. He was hated by some of his fellow nobles who saw him as competition for the Queen's favours.

Queen Mary frequently visited Darnley at Kirk o' Field and, on certain evenings, even slept there although on a different floor level. However, on 9 February, as he was feeling much recovered, it was arranged that the King should move back to Holyroodhouse the following day. It so happened that one of the Queen's pages, Bastien Pages, was to be married and the Queen had been invited to the celebrations. She attended the wedding banquet in the afternoon and afterwards proceeded to Kirk o' Field to see her husband. Mary returned to Holyroodhouse in the evening for the continuation of the nuptial celebrations and the traditional bedding of the bride and groom. At the conclusion of the festivities, the Queen retired to her own bed at Holyroodhouse.

A little while later Mary heard a terrific explosion which rocked the whole of Edinburgh. It was reported to Mary that the house at Kirk o' Field had been blown up with gunpowder. Her immediate thought was for the fate of her husband, the King. Upon investigation, Darnley's body was not found beneath the rubble caused by the explosion, but in an adjacent garden – half-naked and strangled. His corpse was carried indoors for examination by the lords and apothecaries.

Although the matter was never proven, the popular theory which quickly spread was that the Earl of Bothwell was the person behind Darnley's murder. Did the Queen of Scots collude with Bothwell and his accomplices over the assassination? Alas, we shall never know.

Mary appeared distraught at what had happened. Had the explosion been planned to kill her as well? It was only by chance that she had not been sleeping at Kirk o' Field that evening. The Queen of Scots went into mourning for her husband and confined herself to Holyroodhouse, then on medical advice moved to Seton House (B7) for a short stay, to be closer to sea air and get away from the smokey town – Edinburgh was not called Auld Reekie for nothing. The sights and smells of the old town would have been more than insanitary to say the least. Sewage would be emptied from windows of tenement blocks and run down the open gutters to the North Loch below the Castle rock.

During her absence Mary left James in the joint care of Bothwell and Huntly. Rumours raged that Queen Mary and Bothwell had become lovers and together arranged the murder of the King. The Queen blatantly showered Bothwell with gifts and consulted him on all matters of state. Once again, Mary was ruled from her heart rather than her head. It was also noticed how she had taken little action to bring Darnley's murderers to justice. This responsibility was given to his father, the Earl of Lennox, who immediately pointed his finger at Bothwell. However, when he realised the strength of military support that the Borderer had in Edinburgh, Lennox decided not to appear at the enquiry into the murder on 12 April for fear of his own life. In the absence of sufficient evidence to condemn him, Bothwell was acquitted.

The relationship between Queen Mary and Bothwell intensified and he urged her to marry him. Undoubtedly, she was not only becoming attracted to him physically but was being drawn into a much closer personal liaison. The Earl, however, was a married man, though his arranged marriage had been to improve his own fortunes rather than secure a happy family life. Lady Bothwell was happy not to stand in her husband's way when he asked her for a divorce, and she started proceedings on the grounds of his adultery with a servant girl.

Mary arrived in Stirling on 21 April to visit her son, now ten months old. Two days later, she set off on her return to Edinburgh and stayed the night at Linlithgow. Next morning, as the entourage reached the Bridge of Almond, west of Edinburgh, they were suddenly confronted by Bothwell who had with him an army of 800 men. He seized the Queen's bridle and told her that, due to danger that lurked in Edinburgh, he would escort her to Dunbar Castle, a safer haven. Despite protestations from some of her supporters, Mary Queen of Scots went with him willingly. They reached Dunbar at midnight and the gates were made fast.

What happened next is open to speculation. There was talk of abduction, rape, ravishment and a ready willingness on Mary's part. Whatever the truth of the matter, the relationship became intimate.

Whilst the Queen was at Dunbar, a bond was signed by Argyll, Morton and Atholl to attempt to rescue her. In the meantime, Lady Bothwell was granted her divorce early in May and Bothwell received an annulment of the marriage. Through the Protestant Church's divorce procedure, the way was now clear for him to marry his Queen. A request for the banns to be read out for a Protestant marriage between them was refused. Mary bestowed the Dukedom of Orkney upon her lover and announced to her Privy Council that he had been forgiven for abducting her. She had now decided to marry him. Mary and Bothwell set off on for Edinburgh and on 5 May stayed at Hailes Castle (B9) in East Lothian.

The now-ruined Hailes Castle overlooking the River Tyne had been held by the Hepburns from the 14th century. Originally a fortified manor house, it was extended in the 14th and 15th centuries. It contains two vaulted dungeons and a fine 16th-century chapel. The castle changed hands several times during the raids of the Rough Wooing in the 1540s. In 1650 it was laid waste by order of Cromwell but still stands proudly between East Linton and Haddington.

Her third marriage was undoubtedly Mary's gravest mistake. The ceremony took place on 15 May 1567, conducted by Bothwell's friend, the Bishop of Orkney, in the Great Hall of the Palace of Holyroodhouse. The atmosphere was not of celebration but of pending misery. The Queen was depressed and assured the French ambassador that, although she had married according to the Protestant faith, she had not forsaken her own Roman Catholic religion.

The situation amongst the lords grew much more serious. Twenty-six of them banded together to form the Confederate Lords with the specific aim of rescuing Mary from Bothwell's domination and bringing Darnley's murderers to justice.

Within three weeks of marrying Bothwell, Mary Stuart realised the strength of opposition to her recent actions. Not only her Scottish supporters opposed the marriage but also the courts of France, Spain and other European countries whom she had always regarded as allies. Public opinion swiftly moved against Mary and it was widely spread about that she herself had been involved in the King's murder. A placard was placed on the gates of Holyroodhouse which said 'Wantons marry in the month of May'. The flames of suspicion were fanned but the resolve of loyalists to her cause was strengthened. They were convinced that Mary needed to be rescued from Bothwell's evil influence before irreparable damage was done to her reputation – and their own. The Queen quickly discovered that her new husband was also quite unsuitable as a Consort. The Confederate Lords started to plot how they might overthrow Bothwell.

Not long after the wedding Mary and Bothwell moved to Borthwick Castle (B4) under the protection of the 6th Lord Borthwick who had put the building at their disposal. In an effort to free their Queen, a force of some 1,000 men, led by Lord Home, marched on the castle. There was little the royal couple could do except negotiate with the Lords. Whilst Mary Queen of Scots addressed them, Bothwell slipped quietly away unnoticed, knowing full well that capture for him would mean certain death. Early the following morning, disguised as a page boy, Queen Mary climbed through a window of the Great Hall and was lowered by rope to the ground below. She set off through the postern gate and across the glen in search of Bothwell. Mary got lost in the early morning mist but managed to find her way to Cakemuir Castle (B5), a few kilometres to the south on Fala Moor. Cakemuir Castle dates from about 1420 and the four-storey tower was built in 1560 for Adam Wauchope, an advocate, whose coat of arms can still be seen. The house is well preserved and is privately-owned.

At Cakemuir she was made welcome by the Wauchope family, friends of Bothwell. A message was sent to the Earl and the couple were soon re-united. They rode off to Dunbar Castle, a much safer hiding place.

During their short time at Dunbar, every effort was made by them to rally an army and they set off for Edinburgh in mid-June, spending the night at Seton House. It was to be their last night together. Next morning, on 15 June, the opposing sides met at Carberry Hill (B3), near Musselburgh. Even at that point, it was not too late for Mary to withdraw, as the French ambassador had been invited to negotiate between the two sides. If the Queen would disown Bothwell, she would be acknowledged as Sovereign. She refused. Battle commenced and the fighting dragged on. Eventually, the Queen's force began to weaken and drift away. Gradually, her supporters were overcome. Not wishing to see Bothwell killed, she at last offered to submit to the demands of the Confederate Lords. The condition she imposed was that she would dismiss Bothwell if they restored her to her position. Her husband of only four weeks was given his orders to leave. Before doing so, he handed the Queen the document drawn up at Craigmillar Castle between Morton and Maitland and the other conspirators stating their intention of murdering Darnley. Bothwell then rode off towards Dunbar. He and Mary had seen each other for the last time.

James Hepburn, Earl of Bothwell, Consort to Mary Queen of Scots, managed to escape and tried to rally support. A price of 1,000 crowns was placed upon his head for his capture. He moved to the north-east to try and gain the support of Lord Huntly, but failed. He was forced to withdraw to Spynie Palace (B57) to stay with his great-uncle, the Bishop of Moray. After being betrayed, he headed for Orkney, of which he had earlier been created Duke, in a further effort to raise a military force. Still pursued by the Confederate Lords, Bothwell was forced to flee the country. He managed to escape to Norway but was eventually captured and taken to Bergen on 2 September 1567. By the end of the month he had been moved to Copenhagen Castle in Denmark, the start of a ten-year period of being moved from one cold Danish prison to another. Eventually he was transferred to Dragsholm Castle in 1572 (spelt Draugsholm at the time). He had already spent five years in various dungeons. The safe and solid castle was a prison for the nobility.

Since being seriously wounded in the Border affray near Hermitage Castle six years earlier, Bothwell had gangrene in his lower left arm and hand. He suffered greatly from the pain and was described as being insane. This is probably the reason why he tried to commit suicide by banging his head against the stone walls of his cell. He was therefore fastened to a chain and tied to a heavy iron ring in the centre of his cell. Queen Elizabeth sent one of Bothwell's personal enemies, Captain John Clark, with orders to bring Bothwell back to the Tower of London on a charge of high treason – or just his head! If he failed, he was to deliver his own. He failed, and as King Frederik II of Denmark wanted no trouble, John Clark was arrested and thrown into Dragsholm Castle in 1577. He died within the same week as Bothwell in April 1578.

The Castle Governor was Franz Lauridssøn. He decided that, as the body of the Earl smelled so abominable with gangrene and John Clark had suffered from syphilis, especially on his face, only one funeral should be held with one reasonable-looking body. He took the head of Bothwell and the body of Clark and the remaining bones were thrown out onto a moor. These were discovered in excavations during the Second World War.

Until 1970, the mummified body could be seen by visitors in Fårevejle Church near Dragsholm lying in a coffin with a glass lid. Unfortunately, the body was eventually destroyed through light and air which seeped into the glass case. As a result, a distant descendant of Bothwell asked the Danish Queen, Margrethe II, if her ancestor could be properly buried. The corpse was put in a large wooden coffin and placed in Riis' Chapel, an annexe of the Church. The coffin is still on display and information boards relate the story.

Dragsholm Castle is situated at Hørve in the north-western part of Zealand in Denmark. It was built in the 13th century as a bishop's castle and was an enormous Roman-style fortress, as can still be seen from the masonry. After the Reformation, Dragsholm came under the Danish Crown, and until the mid-17th century the castle and estate were granted as a fief. A fief was an estate held on condition of military service by the leading men of the country. Among them was Arild Huitfeld who wrote large parts of *The Chronicle of the History of Denmark* at the castle. The lord-lieutenants and courtiers lived in princely style, but life was hardly as pleasant for some of the other inmates. It was also a gaol for prominent state prisoners, and in the dungeons languished people the King wanted out of sight or with whom he did not know what to do. The most famous of them all was Bothwell.

For centuries, Dragsholm was one of the strongest fortresses in Denmark and it withstood many attacks and sieges. However, the war with Sweden at the end of the 17th century ended in disaster for Denmark and large parts of the stronghold were destroyed. It was re-built between 1694 and 1697 and large parts of the medieval structure were preserved. Reconstruction was carried out by Christian Frederick Adeler, son of a naval hero, and the castle was his family seat for 250 years. Over recent years it has been used extensively for conferences and other functions and overnight accommodation.

Mary Queen of Scots was now a prisoner of the Confederate Lords and taken back to Edinburgh where she was the target of verbal abuse and insults. There were shouts of 'Murderess', 'Prostitute' and 'Adultress' from the townsfolk as she was conducted up the High Street towards the castle. As she rode across the castle drawbridge, the awful realisation of what she had done must have hit her. She had made a very grave mistake but she was unable to turn the clock back. Scotland's reigning monarch had now become a prisoner of her own people.

CHAPTER 10

King James VI of Scotland

ALTHOUGH THE QUEEN HAD been taken prisoner, the government of Scotland had to continue. The Confederate Lords quickly seized power and decided what their next move should be. They were on dangerous ground concerning Mary's imprisonment as she herself had only surrendered at Carberry Hill in an effort to maintain peace. What she anticipated was that there would be a full enquiry into the circumstances surrounding Darnley's murder. In order for state affairs to continue and to carry out their plans, the rebel Lords needed to move Mary Stuart well away from Edinburgh where her presence might be a threat to their plans. The Queen was hurriedly taken from Edinburgh Castle to the house of the Provost of Edinburgh, opposite the Kirk of St Giles in the High Street, where she spent a wretched night as a prisoner. Her appearance at the window incited some citizens to riot, mock, and shout insults at their Queen. Some, however, showed a little respect and compassion. Mary was only too glad to be moved back to Holyroodhouse where she was able to meet up with her ladies-in-waiting.

Loch Leven Castle

She was under the impression that she was to be taken to Stirling Castle to be re-united with her son, James. That, at least, would be some compensation. However, when the Lords arrived with their escort of guards, the entourage left and turned in the direction of the port of Leith (B1). A boat was waiting to take them across the Firth of Forth to the Kingdom of Fife. 'Perhaps', she thought to herself, 'they are taking me to my favourite palace at Falkland.' Such dreams...

Mary was quickly disillusioned as the party crossed the hills and approached the little town of Kinross. A boatman was waiting on the shore of Loch Leven to ferry the royal party to the island fortress of Loch Leven Castle (B38), where the Queen of Scots had stayed in happier times.

On reaching the island, the Queen was ushered into the castle and through into the main reception hall where the castle's owner, Sir William Douglas, was waiting to meet her. Sir William, in the opinion of the rebel Lords, was the ideal choice of gaoler as he was Moray's half-brother, nephew of the Earl of Mar, and cousin to Lord Morton. Being a state prison, documentation had first to be drawn up to confirm the Queen's imprisonment at Loch Leven Castle. Most of her escorts left the very next day, leaving her in the care of Lords Ruthven and Lindsay and, of course, Sir William.

Other members of the Douglas family were living at Loch Leven Castle whilst Mary was held prisoner. There was Sir William's mother, the Lady Margaret Douglas, née Erskine, the former mistress of James V and mother of the illegitimate James Stewart, and another of her sons, George Douglas, a debonair and good-looking individual. Mary Seton was allowed to re-join the Queen at Loch Leven in September 1567.

Despite her royal status, Queen Mary, though treated courteously, had to endure the discomfort of life at such a bleak location. She was now living at the centre of a windswept loch. Mary was also in the early stages of another pregnancy and her health was far from good. From the time of her arrival she had been in a state of nervous exhaustion, but after two weeks she began to feel better.

Mary had been assured by Secretary Maitland that if she divorced Bothwell, she would be fully restored to her throne. Bearing in mind that she was expecting another child, there was no way that she would compromise the baby's position before it was born by agreeing to such an arrangement which would mean that if she divorced, the child would be declared illegitimate.

Clearly, the Confederate Lords had a problem on their hands over what to do with their captive Queen. Should she be restored to her throne, she would undoubtedly take action against them. On the other hand, Mary's thirteen-month-old son, James, was at Stirling. The thought of handing the throne to the young prince and ruling on his behalf whilst he was still a minor, was an appealing proposition. The more they considered the matter, the more attractive it appeared.

Mary Stuart began to fear for her life and wondered if it might be better for her to return to France to join a religious order. After all, she still had many relatives on her mother's side there. She could perhaps receive shelter from her grandmother, the Duchess Antoinette of Guise, or her aunt Renée at the convent of St Pierre in Rheims. That would be a far better prospect than imprisonment at Loch Leven.

It has been argued that the Queen had become pregnant by Bothwell through his 'abduction' of her at Dunbar the previous April. However, around the middle of July Mary miscarried twins. So that was that! Naturally, this took a toll on the Queen's health and for some time she was in a weak state. It was about this time that Lord Lindsay came with news that orders had been issued by the Privy Council for the Queen to sign a series of documents. These stated she would have to abdicate the throne in favour of her son, Prince James. Once again she refused to accept the demands of the Confederate Lords. Lindsay threatened her with force and possible death if she refused to comply with their wishes. Still she hesitated.

Not everyone on the island was against the Queen. She found she had an ally in the younger brother of Sir William, George

Douglas. He had already incited the servants working in the Douglas household to rebel at the prospect of Mary Stuart being removed to a new prison.

After much consideration and in order to save her life, Mary Queen of Scots finally signed the forms of abdication. She was only twenty-four years old. The Lords of the Congregation then wasted no time in proclaiming the little prince King James VI of Scotland.

Shortly afterwards, on 29 July 1567, James was crowned King in a ceremony which took place at the Church of the Holy Rude – a Protestant church – close to Stirling Castle. He was only thirteen months old. Lord James Stewart, Earl of Moray, was recommended as Regent. On hearing the news at Loch Leven Castle, Mary wept whilst others celebrated.

The Church of the Holy Rude has been Stirling's principal church for over 500 years. It has some magnificent stained glass windows and one of Scotland's few surviving medieval open timber roofs. The nave and tower date from between 1456 and 1470.

Moray returned to Scotland from his exile in England. At last he was on the threshold of achieving the power he had coveted for so long. As Regent for the young King, he could look forward to a good number of years of ruling Scotland himself. One of his first tasks was to visit Loch Leven to meet his half-sister, Mary Stuart. The interview between them was not a good one and he condemned her for past demeanours. As the former Sovereign, Mary asked Moray to take over the Regency of her son now that her own position had become untenable. Moray was subsequently proclaimed Regent of Scotland on 22 August.

Once Mary had become used to the idea of no longer being a reigning monarch, her health and disposition began to improve. With this came an awareness of the affection that the young George Douglas was beginning to show towards her. With her personal charm, she endeared herself to others on the island including Willie Douglas, an orphan who was George's younger cousin and known as 'the foundling'. In addition, Mary knew she could rely on further support from Lord Seton, the Hamilton family and others. What was really at the back of her mind was the possibility of escape to the mainland. This could only be achieved if she had some help from within the confines of her prison.

Although one or two earlier unsuccessful attempts had been made to rescue the Queen, the most opportune situation presented itself on 2 May 1568. Lady Douglas, wife of Sir William and one of Mary's constant companions, gave birth. Young Willie Douglas had organised a few celebrations to commemorate the occasion and this gave the Queen some respite from her normal routine. It was rather like old times at the court of France and the masques the Queen had once enjoyed at Holyroodhouse. During the festivities Mary overhead a conversation that a large party of horsemen, led by Lord Seton, had been spotted on the mainland.

Mary then joined Sir William in his chamber where, from his window, he happened to spot Willie skulking suspiciously around the boats tied up in the tiny harbour. Willie's task was to chain the boats together so that no-one would be able to pursue them. Mary pretended to faint in order to divert Sir William's attention away from Willie's activities.

Later, Mary was given a pearl earring by a servant who stated it had been found in the castle grounds. She knew full well that this was a signal from George Douglas to confirm all was in order. The Queen then had supper which was served to her by Sir William. Once the meal was over, she made the excuse that she was going upstairs to pray. Mary then swiftly made her way to her own apartment to change into an old and threadbare outfit. Meanwhile, Willie Douglas was waiting upon Sir William who was about to commence his own meal. While he was serving, Willie deliberately dropped a napkin over his master's keys. As Sir William by now was becoming a little worse for drink, he failed to notice the youth had picked up the keys as he retrieved the napkin.

Willie quietly left the dining hall and signalled to one of the Queen's ladies that all was well. Mary and her companion quickly followed her young supporter into the courtyard where he unlocked the postern gate. Quietly, they made their way down to where a boatman was waiting to row them across the loch. The Queen was spotted by some washerwomen, but Willie persuaded them to keep quiet. In Mary's absence, Mary Seton acted as a decoy by impersonating the Queen.

According to popular belief, the youth dropped the keys of the castle into the water. The keys were recovered from the loch many years later and came into the possession of Sir Walter Scott and can be seen at his home, Abbotsford, near Melrose.

When the small party reached the far shore, they were met by friends and supporters. Mary Queen of Scots and Willie were mounted on horseback and George Douglas accompanied them to meet up with Lord Seton at a secret location. Seton then conducted them across the Firth of Forth at North Queensferry (B28) and they reached Niddry Castle (B17), one of his family homes, around midnight.

Niddry Castle near Winchburgh, west of Edinburgh, was built by the 3rd Lord Seton in the early 16th century and is a single tower fortification. It stayed in the possession of the Setons until the late 17th century and then passed to the Hope family whilst their new mansion, Hopetoun House, was in the process of being built. Niddry Castle later fell into a state of disrepair and neglect but over recent years has been restored to some of its former glory with financial assistance from the National Trust for Scotland. It is now privately-owned.

Mary Stuart could not believe her luck that, after over ten months of imprisonment at Loch Leven, she was free again. News quickly spread of the Queen's escape and she soon found that many new supporters were rallying to her cause. From Niddry, the royal party rode to Cadzow Castle (B21), close to the town of Hamilton, and the main house of the Hamilton family. Hamilton Palace (B21) was demolished in the 1920s due to subsidence and only the magnificent stable block now remains.

Cadzow Castle is a picturesque ruin which stands above the River Avan, in the Châtelherault Country Park south of Hamilton.

It had originally been a royal residence and the old oak trees in the park are said to have been planted by David I. The Hamiltons received the grant of Cadzow from Robert the Bruce after the Battle of Banockburn in 1314, and maintained the property until the 16th century. After the Queen's defeat later at Langside, the Earl of Moray destroyed the Castle as punishment for Archbishop Hamilton of St Andrews who had supported Mary.

For a few days the Queen used Cadzow Castle as her base and moved between there and nearby Craignethan Castle (B20), another Hamilton residence. Craignethan was comparatively new as it was built in the 16th century by Sir James Hamilton of Finnart, an illegitimate son of the 1st Earl of Arran. Sir James was a talented architect who did much to restore royal palaces at Stirling, Falkland and Linlithgow as well as making improvements to Edinburgh Castle. He was executed by James V in 1540 on a charge of attempted regicide. The Hamiltons were staunch supporters of the Queen of Scots. The original castle was largely dismantled by the Queen's enemies but a new house was built on the site in 1665 by the Hay family.

Mary Queen of Scots called her Council together which by then consisted of Lords Hamilton, Herries, Melville, Livingston and Seton together with George Douglas.

By 8 May solid support was beginning to build. In total, nine bishops, nine lords, eighteen lairds and many others had signed a joint declaration. Meanwhile, the Confederate Lords, led by Moray, were in hot pursuit of their former prisoner and were rallying troops of their own to overcome the Queen and her supporters. However, the royalist group was the stronger of the two forces.

A confrontation between the two sides finally took place at Langside (B22), then a small village just south of Glasgow. The Earl of Moray's troops commenced their attack on the Queen's force which included men supplied by Hamilton, Herries and Argyll. Mary had put Argyll in charge of the operation but he failed to live up to the challenge. As Mary watched the battle from a window of nearby Cathcart Castle (B22), she gazed with melancholy as her supporters were gradually overcome. The Battle of Langside was fought and the Queen lost. Moray had the upper hand.

Cathcart Castle was situated by the White Cart Water and was partly demolished in the 15th century. Only a few ruins remain as it was later replaced by the nearby Cathcart House. The site of the Battle of Langside is commemorated by a large memorial just outside Queen's Park, the first public park opened by Glasgow Corporation and laid out to a landscape design by Sir Joseph Paxton. The lion which surmounts the monument faces the area where Mary's forces gathered before the battle. A nearby district is still called Battlefield.

The Queen knew she must move quickly if she was to avoid re-capture. She left her position overlooking the battleground and, accompanied by Lord Herries and a small group of people, first considered riding to Dumbarton to board a boat for France. It would have meant crossing the Clyde to the north bank and there was no time to do this. A decision was hurriedly made to head for the Solway coast in South-West Scotland where a boat might be obtained.

The party first headed for Sanquhar Castle (C23), then Terregles Castle (C20) near Dumfries. On arrival, they were informed that Moray's forces were in hot pursuit. With no time to waste, they continued their journey to the Abbey of Dundrennan (C16) not far from Kirkcudbright.

Sanquhar Castle was a substantial castle with a courtyard which was built by the Crichton family in the Middle Ages. The most conspicuous features today are the outer ditches, the gatehouse range and the restored tower house. Terregles is three kilometres north-west of Dumfries and the original castle was rebuilt in its present form in 1789. Nearby Terregles church has a restored choir dating from 1583 with several interesting tombs and stalls. Dundrennan Abbey was founded by David I and Fergus, Lord of Galloway, for the Cistercian order around 1142. It was annexed to the Chapel Royal at Stirling in 1621. Much of the building today is irretrievably ruined but there are remains of the 13th-century Chapter House and parts of the transepts. It is debatable whether Mary actually stayed within the confines of the Abbey or in a nearby house not far from the main buildings.

Mary called together members of her Council within the Abbey. Although it was well fortified, they could not afford to stay there if they were to avoid being overcome by Moray's army. Discussion took place as to where they should go and the majority felt that France would be a far safer place for their Queen in her present situation. She might also gather much military strength through her own family, the Guises, and their many other Catholic supporters. Stubbornly, Mary refused to follow this course and insisted they should cross to England and appeal to her royal cousin. Queen Elizabeth might be willing to supply her with the necessary troops to overcome Moray. Members of the Council were astounded at her decision as Moray had earlier been given shelter by Elizabeth and had built up a regular dialogue with the English Queen. This, they advised, would be a most unwise move. Yet Mary could not be persuaded otherwise.

The only alternative left open to her supporters was to accompany the Queen of Scots into England. A message was forwarded by Lord Herries to Sir Richard Lowther, the Deputy Governor of Carlisle Castle, to inform him of the Queen's intentions. He requested a safe passage for the Queen and her friends.

On 15 May 1568, just a fortnight after her escape from Loch Leven Castle, Mary Queen of Scots boarded a fishing boat at the mouth of the nearby Abbey burn, known today as Port Mary (C17). In the bay of Port Mary is a boulder from which the Queen reputedly stepped into the boat. From there she crossed the Solway Firth, bound for the Cumberland coast of England. As the little boat moved towards the English shore, Mary began to have second thoughts. Unfortunately, the tide and strong currents in the estuary did not allow them to return to the Scottish coast. They would have to continue their journey towards the Cumbrian mountains which loomed high in the distance. Little did Mary realise that she was sailing into captivity which was to last to the end of her days.

CHAPTER 11

England and Captivity

MARY QUEEN OF SCOTS, by crossing into England, had unknowingly committed herself to a lifetime of imprisonment during which her status and conditions would steadily deteriorate. She must have had mixed feelings as the fishing boat left Scottish shores behind. Were Moray and his army far behind? Would they follow her into England? What sort of reception was she likely to receive from Elizabeth? Would she, after all, have been better leaving for France? What about her little son, the new King James? Would he be in safe hands? What would they tell him about his mother as he grew older? Would she ever see him again? These must have been painful thoughts as she pondered her future.

On the other hand, if she went to France, what might that hold? First, there was her formidable mother-in-law, Catherine de Medici, who still ruled the roost at the French court. Mary had not won any friends in France through the events surrounding her second and third marriages. Her own family were the only real supporters on

Bolton Castle, Wensleydale

whom she could rely, but even they were likely to use her again for their own political ends. There were so many imponderables that Mary felt she had made the right decision in going to England.

Mary Stuart, when she came to consider Elizabeth, foolishly thought that as they were blood relations and of the same status, the English Queen would receive her as a long lost sister. Surely she should have realised that blood relations can often prove the worst of enemies. Had not her relationship with James Stewart, Earl of Moray, already taught her that lesson? She had never met Elizabeth in person. Contact between the two Queens had always been by correspondence or through others. Mary could only surmise what Elizabeth was like. Perhaps the English Queen would receive her warmly and offer military support to overcome the rebels? That would allow her to return to Scotland.

What Mary Queen of Scots had forgotten to take into account was that Elizabeth was a Protestant and she a Roman Catholic. That and the English Queen's continuing stigma of alleged illegitimacy were two of the main stumbling blocks.

Mary first set foot on English soil at Workington where she was conducted to Workington Hall (c18). She was given hospitality by the Curwen family. Sir Henry Curwen happened to be in London at the time but had informed Lord Herries that his house was at the Queen's disposal. Lady Curwen provided Mary with some of her clothes, as all Mary had when she arrived at Workington were those she was wearing. As a token of her gratitude, Mary gave to Lady Curwen a small agate wine cup, still in the possession of the family today. The Earl of Northumberland paid the Queen a visit at Workington. She felt she had an ally as he also was a Catholic. However, he had already been given instructions by Elizabeth that the Queen of Scots must be closely observed. Naively, Mary was under the impression that the guards were merely for her own safety.

Workington Hall had been occupied since the early 13th century but the first stone building on the site, a typical Border peel tower, was erected by Gilbert de Cluwen in 1362. Further fortifications were added in 1380 with a barbican, gatehouse and bat-tlemented curtain walls. An undercroft and kitchen were added in 1404, followed by a great hall with a high pitched roof. It was in a room on the first floor of the north wing that Mary spent the night of 16 May 1568. From this room, the Queen of Scots wrote her famous letter to Elizabeth to inform her of her plight. She also appealed for military assistance to help win back the throne of Scotland from Moray and his rebel lords. The letter, written in French, contained the following words:

> I entreat you to send for me as soon as possible, for I am in a pitiable condition, not only for a Queen but for a gen-tlewoman, having nothing in the world but the clothes in which I escaped, riding sixty miles in the first day, and not daring to travel afterwards except by night, as I hope to be able to show you, if it please you to have compassion on my great misfortunes, and to permit me to come and bewail them to you.
>
> Not to weary you I will now pray to God to give you health and a long and happy life, and to myself patience, and that consolation I await from you to whom I present my humble commendations.
>
> From Workington, this 17th day of May.
>
> Your very faithful and affectionate good sister and cousin and escaped prisoner
>
> MARIE R.

Later that same day, Mary and her party bade farewell to her hostess, Lady Curwen. The Earl of Northumberland escorted the Queen to Cockermouth Hall (C19) where they stayed as guests of Master Henry Fletcher, a wealthy merchant of the town. In Cockermouth she had visits from several members of the nobility including Lady Scrope, sister to the Duke of Norfolk. Mary received confirmation that, for the time being, Carlisle Castle (E6) was to be put at her disposal and they moved there the following day.

Carlisle, an ancient Border fortress, has been a natural defensive site as far back as the Romans and Saxons, and for hundreds of years was the butt of continuing warfare between the Scots and the English. William Rufus claimed the fort for England in 1092 and began building the present castle which was continually strengthened throughout the Middle Ages. David 1 of Scotland captured Carlisle in 1138 as he marched south in support of his niece, Empress Matilda, daughter of Henry 1 in her war against Stephen for the English crown. After his defeat, he fled back to Carlisle and died in 1153, four years after knighting Matilda's son, the future Henry 11. Henry built the walls and keep which still stand today. Edward I used Carlisle as a base during his campaigns against Scotland and held Parliaments in the town. During the Civil War, Carlisle held out for the King. It was besieged by Scottish troops in 1644, and surrendered the following year. The castle became the last stronghold in English history to succumb to military attack. In 1745, the Young Pretender's garrison – left behind during the retreat from Derby – exchanged a few shots with the Duke of Cumberland's forces before capitulating. Carlisle Castle today is well preserved; stones mark the lower courses of the original Queen Mary's Tower, and a wooden dining table, at which Mary celebrated Mass, is on view.

Mary Queen of Scots arrived at Carlisle on 18 May. As a matter of courtesy, the Deputy Governor of the Castle, Sir Richard Lowther, wrote to Elizabeth's Private Secretary, Sir William Cecil. He informed him of the Queen of Scots' arrival, suggesting that she be detained in Carlisle until Elizabeth had been given sufficient time to appraise the matter and issue further commands. The Governor of the Castle, Lord Scrope, was away at the English court at the time so, for the present, Lowther had to take on the responsibility himself. Lowther was, of course, suspicious of Mary Stuart's motives. Outwardly, he treated her with the utmost courtesy as befitted a Queen. Privately, he considered her a political prisoner of his own sovereign.

Even though every comfort was made available to make

Mary's stay as pleasant as possible, her movements were discreetly kept in check by Lowther. The Castle was a forbidding place, though the Queen was becoming used to living in uncomfortable dwellings. Lady Scrope, who had accompanied Mary from Cockermouth, was appointed to attend her, and they not only became friends but also found they had much in common. For a start, they were both Roman Catholics. Whilst she was at Carlisle, Mary was allowed to retain nearly forty of her followers and servants. These included George and Willie Douglas and David Beaton, and she was re-joined by Mary Seton – the last remaining of the original four Maries.

A few days later, Lord Scrope returned from London, accompanied by Sir Francis Knollys, Elizabeth's counsellor. Knollys brought with him the news that Elizabeth forwarded messages of sympathy at her royal cousin's plight and assured the Queen of Scots of her friendship and favour. She had also issued commands that Mary and her escorts be treated with all honour and courtesy. In addition, her servants and subjects should be given free access to speak with their Queen whilst at Carlisle whenever they wished.

In practice, these orders were never adhered to and it soon became obvious to Mary and her supporters that obstacles were being placed in their way to prevent such freedom of movement. Elizabeth knew full well, even at that early stage, that Mary Stuart would soon become a rallying point for plots by Roman Catholics in England, Scotland and countries on the Continent. She could not be trusted.

Elizabeth was faced with a dilemma. On the one hand, she professed her sympathy at Mary having lost her Scottish throne so she publicly offered her refuge in England. But in private, she knew that the shadow of illegitimacy which surrounded her own birth meant that Mary Stuart had a strong claim on the English throne through her maternal grandmother, Margaret Tudor.

To be practical, Elizabeth must treat her royal charge as a prisoner but never describe her as such. She was to be referred to as a foreign Queen who was on a sojourn in England pending return to her own country of Scotland. In reality, Mary Queen of Scots was to be guarded, watched and kept in secure detention until Elizabeth and her ministers decided exactly how to handle her royal cousin.

During her stay at Carlisle Castle, Mary witnessed what might have been the first international game of football when twenty of her French and Scottish followers were challenged by Lord Scrope's English servants. Although the result was never recorded, the game was reported to have lasted for two hours.

Despite letters written to Elizabeth pleading for assistance, Mary was given the news that she could not be received at court. There was no chance of this whilst she was still under suspicion over the murder of her second husband, Lord Darnley, and the fact that she had married his alleged murderer, Bothwell. In addition, the English Queen considered Carlisle Castle far too close to the Scottish border for Mary's safety and security. She must be moved to a more suitable place of confinement without further delay.

Unknown to Mary, a number of letters written in French had been discovered at a house in Edinburgh. These were allegedly written by Mary to Bothwell whilst she was in Glasgow. Moray was having them translated as evidence against his half-sister. If he was proven correct, they would implement her in Darnley's murder. Elizabeth was aware of this.

After six weeks at Carlisle, Mary Queen of Scots was moved via Wharton and Lowther Castle (E7) to Bolton Castle (E8) where she arrived on 15 July. Bolton Castle was a remote fortress standing on the northern slopes of lovely Wensleydale in the former North Riding of Yorkshire. It was built by Richard, 1st Lord Scrope, in the late 14th century. On the accession of Richard II, Scrope was appointed Steward of the Royal Household and later given the Chancellorship of England. In 1537, the Abbot of Jervaulx sought sanctuary in the castle when his abbey was threatened during the rising of the Pilgrimage of Grace. After the defeat of the King's army at Marston Moor in 1644 during the Civil Wars, Bolton

Castle was held for the King by John Scrope. The siege lasted more than a year before the garrison finally surrendered. Though now mainly in ruins, the building is a high walled fortress with large square towers at each corner, and still shows many traces of the time when Mary Queen of Scots stayed within its confines. Over recent years efforts have been made to interpret the history of the castle and its part in Mary's life. It has a number of tableaux and other effects which help the visitor re-live its history.

It was whilst Mary was at Bolton Castle under the custody of Lord Scrope that the Conference of York (E9) took place in October 1568. This was mainly an enquiry into the reasons for Mary being deposed from her Scottish throne by her nobles. Moray was named as the chief instigator. In reality, Elizabeth was seeking justification for holding the Queen of Scots a prisoner in England. Should she be proved to have been involved in Darnley's murder, then Elizabeth would accept the reasoning for her deposition from the Scottish throne. Commissioners from Scotland were allowed to attend along with those from England, led by the Duke of Norfolk, who were acting on behalf of Elizabeth.

Whilst these enquiries were taking place, the so-called Casket Letters were first produced as evidence. They implicated Mary in Darnley's murder and were allegedly written to Bothwell in her own hand. The Queen of Scots denied having written the letters and proclaimed they were forgeries by persons unknown. The case was never proven and the truth of the matter and the authorship of the letters may never be known. They have remained one of the on-going mysteries surrounding Mary Queen of Scots which have been debated down the years.

Elizabeth remained unimpressed by the Scottish lords who, she realised, were determined to convict their Queen. Mary was, after all, born a royal princess like herself and should be acknowledged as such whatever her faults. However, if Elizabeth let her go free, she could well rally Catholic supporters and bring about an uprising in Northern England. The Queen of Scots might also seek support from France and Spain to make a bid for the English throne. To protect herself, Elizabeth was adamant that her Scottish rival should not be allowed to leave England for fear that she would rally foreign support. By the beginning of 1569, it had become clear that no satisfactory decision would be reached from the Conference of York or a later one held at Westminster on the same subject. The English commissioners had come to the conclusion that the royal prisoner must be held securely but, at the same time, be treated with the courtesies due to a queen.

As the weeks passed at Bolton Castle, Mary Stuart began to realise the impossible situation in which she was now placed. She confided in her hostess, Lady Scrope, and found that there was some sympathy for her case from members of the English nobility. One of these was Lady Scrope's brother, the Duke of Norfolk. He was six years older than Mary, the leading peer in the realm, and one of the wealthiest men in England. He was also a widower and a Roman Catholic. Being a man of ambition, he would have seized on an opportunity to make contact with the Queen of Scots. Bearing in mind her claims to the English throne, he could well see himself as a possible suitor should anything happen to Bothwell or Mary's marriage be annulled.

Letters were being smuggled in to Mary from George Douglas who by now had left her employ. She received assurances of support from the King of France and her uncle, the Cardinal of Lorraine. In Scotland, Moray had upset many people and Huntly and Argyll were ready to take up arms again on Mary's behalf. Lord Herries had had a meeting with Elizabeth who was now willing to help reinstate Mary as Queen in Scotland. This, however, would only be under certain conditions. Mary must sever all contact with France, forbid the Mass to be celebrated in Scotland and renounce all claim to the English throne. Mary Stuart would be placed in an impossible position if she accepted the terms. She would be completely reliant on Elizabeth who, in turn, could not be trusted.

Mary was cheered when she was secretly informed that plans were in hand to effect her release. Only a small number of the Queen's supporters were aware of the plans including the ever-faithful Willie Douglas who was again a leading player in the proposed escape. The idea was that the Queen would be let down through a window of Bolton Castle along with Mary Seton. Horses would be waiting to take them back to the Scottish border and on to Ferniehirst Castle near Jedburgh which could become a rallying point for the Queen's armies.

At the appointed time, Mary was safely lowered to the ground from a window in the north-west tower. She was followed by one of her servants who fell, disturbing the guards. Seconds later, the Queen of Scots was confronted by her gaoler, Lord Scrope. The plot had failed.

Once the news of the attempted escape reached the English court, Elizabeth conferred with her ministers, William Cecil and the Earl of Leicester. They decided that Bolton Castle was too dangerous a location for Mary Queen of Scots to be kept as it still offered easy access to Scotland. They criticised the lack of security there and decided that the captive must be moved further into England under a new gaoler. Someone would be needed who had resources, properties, and estates which were far enough away from Scotland or any seaport which might allow easy access to or from countries on the Continent.

The choice of gaoler fell on George Talbot, 6th Earl of Shrewsbury, and arrangements were made to transfer Mary into his custody without further delay. The dejected Queen of Scots left the lofty heights of Bolton Castle for her journey south. The party, with a strong force of guards, travelled via Ripon, Wetherby, Pontefract, Rotherham, Walton Hall near Chesterfield, South Wingfield and Derby. Her next prison was not only to break her health but also her spirit. Mary Queen of Scots was desolate in the extreme.

CHAPTER 12

The Shrewsbury Years

THE EARL AND COUNTESS of SHREWSBURY received Mary Queen of Scots into her new prison at Tutbury Castle (F10) in Staffordshire. The meeting was significant in that it introduced into Mary's life the forceful character of the Countess of Shrewsbury, better known throughout history as the formidable Bess of Hardwick. In many ways she was not unlike Mary's first mother-in-law, Catherine de Medici.

Bess was known as a proud, arrogant and domineering woman, ruthless in her ambitions and determined to have her own way despite the cost to herself or her family. She also had similar traits to Queen Elizabeth in her stubbornness and masculine approach. The main difference between them was that Bess was four times married whereas Elizabeth had never taken a husband.

Through her three previous marriages, Bess had become a very wealthy woman. She was born in 1518 at Hardwick Hall (F3) in

Wingfield Manor

Derbyshire and had first been married at the tender age of four-teen to Robert Barley, a local squire. The marriage was shortlived as her husband died whilst still in his teens, leaving Bess a rich widow. She soon re-married and chose a much older man for her second husband, Sir William Cavendish, and it was by him that she had her children. Despite their differences in age, the marriage seems to have been successful. Sir William bought Chatsworth in Derbyshire and began to rebuild it. Unfortunately, he died whilst initial work was being carried out, leaving Bess to make arrange-ments for its completion. It was during that time that she first acquired a taste for building noble houses, a passion in which she indulged to her dying day.

By the time of Sir William's death, Bess had become used to life at the English court and found herself a third husband in William St Loe, another wealthy nobleman who was considerably older than his bride. That marriage was also shortlived and he died leav-ing Bess a small fortune.

It was really through her ambitions for the betterment of her family that she agreed to a fourth marriage. She promised to marry George Talbot, Earl of Shrewsbury, on one condition – that two of his children would marry two of her own by her second husband. These alliances would not only provide for her own future well-being but also secure unions for her children with illus-trious families of the British nobility. In so doing, Bess set up a dynasty which has continued down the generations through many noble houses. Bess's eldest son, Henry Cavendish, and her youngest daughter, Mary, were therefore married to Shrewsbury's eldest daughter, Grace Talbot, and his second son, Gilbert. These marriages are recorded in the registers at Sheffield Parish Church (FI), now the Anglican Cathedral, and the date was February 1568.

Bess had been married to Shrewsbury less than a year when they were commissioned by Queen Elizabeth to take on the task of guarding Mary Queen of Scots. The Earl, eight years younger than Bess, was under the influence of his ambitious wife. Mary, twenty years younger than Bess, may first have looked on her as a matriarchal figure. Bess may have reciprocated by showing signs of a maternal attitude towards their new ward.

Tutbury Castle is a motte and bailey castle set on top of a hill overlooking the flatlands of Needwood Forest. There was a castle on the site at the time of the Norman Conquest and from 1086 to 1265 it belonged to the Ferrers family, the Earls of Derby. The castle was visited by Henry III in 1251 and by Queen Eleanor in 1257. However, in 1266 when Robert, Earl of Derby joined with the barons in their rebellion against Henry III, he lost Tutbury to Edmund, the King's younger son. Edmund became Earl of Lancaster and Tutbury remained the property of his descendants, the Earls and Dukes of Lancaster. Since 1399, it has belonged to the Sovereign as part of the Duchy of Lancaster. It is now a stately ruin which sits on top of rather a steep hill close to the Norman priory church of St Mary. There are splendid views across Needwood Forest, once part of a huge forest which covered central England in the 12th century and where a number of the Robin Hood legends originated.

Tutbury Castle must have appeared a stark, forbidding place to Mary and her entourage as they approached it from the little town of Tutbury on 4 February 1569. They would have wound their way up the hill to cross the drawbridge and pass through the gatehouse into the castle. From the high towers – a local landmark – it would have been easy to spot anyone approaching.

How right Mary was concerning Tutbury. Although every courtesy was bestowed on her, it was cold and draughty. She could not have arrived at a worse time of the year, it being the middle of winter, and it soon proved to be the bleakest residence she had ever lived in. Initially, she was lodged in the south range of buildings where the hall and great chamber were divided with a wainscot partition. Mary spent most of her time within the confines of the castle. Her horses and those of her supporters were stabled in the nearby town.

Though, on the surface, Bess treated the royal guest with concern for her comfort and well-being, underneath she approached her with caution and suspicion. Yet Bess would be careful that she did not appear unfriendly. After all, she must have realised that it was not beyond the bounds of possibility that Mary Queen of Scots might one day inherit the English throne, especially if Elizabeth were overthrown, assassinated or died childless. With her instinct for self-protection and preservation, Bess would be anxious to safeguard her future, regardless of who occupied the English throne.

Lord Shrewsbury was much more kindly disposed toward his charge and made every effort to try and provide for her comforts. He immediately set about writing to Elizabeth to inform her of the bleak conditions. Soon, extra furnishings and comforts were despatched from the Tower of London to Tutbury Castle. Even so, the cold and severity of conditions soon made Queen Mary ill. Rheumatism began to creep into her bones and this troubled her for the rest of her life. She developed a fever, but before he dare move his ward to one of his more comfortable residences, Shrewsbury knew that he must seek Elizabeth's approval. He wrote to his Queen and, in due course, permission was granted for the removal of the royal prisoner to a new residence — Wingfield Manor (F6), another Shrewsbury house in Derbyshire.

Shrewsbury had, however, made one unfortunate mistake. He had not informed his wife, the Countess. When she heard of the arrangements, Bess flew into a rage and accused him of having become besotted with Mary Stuart. The Earl naturally denied this but Bess was adamant. From that point on, jealousy over their wardship of the Queen of Scots crept into their relationship. It was the start of much bitterness between them and would, eventually, lead to a complete marriage breakdown whilst Mary was in their custody.

It must have come as a blessed relief when Mary and her retinue left Tutbury, bound for Wingfield Manor, a much more pleasant place. A favourite of the Shrewsburys, it stood on a hilltop overlooking a valley through which flows the meandering River Amber on its way to the Trent.

Wingfield Manor, now a fine ruin, was once a palace built by Ralph, Lord Cromwell, Treasurer to Henry VI, and has an imposing array of towers and chimneys. In 1429, Lord Cromwell acquired the site from rival claimants and ten years later began rebuilding a great hall, kitchen and lodgings at the centre of the old enclosure. A high tower was built across the south-west corner providing a splendid lookout place. In 1455, the property was purchased by the 2nd Earl of Shrewsbury who continued building. It became a magnificent mansion, with two courts, extensive outbuildings and stables around the main block. Beneath the great hall is a perfectly preserved crypt with a vaulted roof.

When Mary Queen of Scots arrived at Wingfield on 20 April 1569, she was given apartments in the north-west tower, with wide views across the valley. As a residence, Mary Stuart must have found it much fairer than Tutbury and this, in itself, must have hastened her recovery from illness. Her friends came and went with more freedom and she wrote many letters.

Had discretion been one of Mary's virtues, she might well have found favour with Elizabeth at this time. However, despite her freedom of movement, she was still being closely watched and guarded. She began to involve herself in treasonable correspondence with the Duke of Alva, Spanish Viceroy in the Low Countries. Thomas Howard, the 4th Duke of Norfolk, had also started writing to Queen Mary. In an effort to build up a relationship, he began by sending gifts of money and then forwarded a diamond ring. One of Mary's callers was John Leslie, Bishop of Ross, Mary's envoy from Scotland. He specified that there was much support from the nobles in both England and Scotland for her marriage to Norfolk. One of these was no less than Robert Dudley, Earl of Leicester, Elizabeth's favourite. There was much rivalry for Elizabeth's favour between Leicester and William Cecil. Cecil had offered his support to the Earl of Moray who, in turn, supported the Protestant Queen Elizabeth. More news brought by the Bishop which delighted Mary was an assurance that an annulment of her marriage with the Earl of Bothwell was possible as

Rome was now in favour. Norfolk could then become her husband. Her spirits began to lift as she saw the possibilities which were opening up.

Unfortunately, Norfolk had an enemy in one Leonard Dacre who had a meeting with Mary at Wingfield when he informed her that his cousins, the Catholic Earls of Northumberland and Westmorland, were in full support of her cause and wished to help. Dacre was fully aware of Norfolk's plans, and in an effort to sabotage them, proposed that Mary should marry Don Juan of Austria, one of her strongest supporters in her claim for the throne of England. A plan was hatched for Mary's escape from Wingfield, and the situation seemed to be working in favour of the conspirators when Shrewsbury had a seizure. During his confinement to bed, security at Wingfield began to slacken which allowed more freedom for letters and visitors.

Due to Shrewsbury's worsening condition, Bess wrote to Elizabeth for permission to move him to the town of Buxton (F8) where he could take the healing spa waters to hasten his recovery. However, the English Queen did not respond to the request so, in her usual bluff way, Bess decided to take matters into her own hands and set about organising to move the Earl to Buxton forthwith.

When news eventually reached the English court that the Shrewsburys had gone to Buxton without permission, Elizabeth was furious and ordered their immediate return to Tutbury where the Queen of Scots was to join them under the escort of the Earl of Huntingdon, a much less kindly gaoler.

At the English court, Leicester, realising his folly, confessed his part in the plot to Elizabeth. He explained that the idea behind the scheme was to marry Mary off to Norfolk. Under pressure, Leicester named his fellow conspirators. Norfolk was then committed to the Tower of London. Orders were sent by Elizabeth that the Queen of Scots' entourage be reduced and she was neither to receive messages nor visitors from the outside world. This time, Mary's apartments at Tutbury were even more primitive than on her first visit. She was placed in rooms overlooking the castle sewers and complained bitterly of the stench when the privies were emptied beneath her window every day. She felt degraded in the extreme.

In November, the Catholic Earls of Northumberland and Westmorland began their uprising, as predicted by Dacre. It seemed to have been doomed from the start and its motives had been religious rather than to secure the escape of the Queen of Scots. Mary herself disapproved of any violence and felt it would do her cause no good whatsoever. The plan had been to take Mary back to Scotland where troops would be raised by her faithful lords in order to restore her to her throne.

As news of the Northern Uprising was received, Mary's new gaoler, Huntingdon, swiftly made arrangements for her removal from Tutbury and she was escorted to Ashby-de-la-Zouch Castle (F15) and then taken on to Coventry (F18).

Ashby-de-la-Zouch Castle in Leicestershire was originally a Norman manor house. Edward IV gave it to the Lord Chamberlain, William, Lord Hastings, as a reward for his part in the Wars of the Roses, and Hastings enlarged and strengthened it. He was beheaded by Richard III for treason but his son restored the family fortunes. Mary Queen of Scots' son, James VI and I, frequently enjoyed great hospitality at the castle. It is now a rambling ruin close to the town centre.

In Coventry Mary lodged at the Black Bull Inn before suitable accommodation was made ready in Caesar's Tower of St Mary's Hall in the town centre. She was kept in a room on the third floor connected to the armoury by a square-headed doorway just 1.5 m. in height. Mary would have had to duck before entering or leaving in order to avoid bumping her forehead. A framed copy of an explanatory letter sent by Queen Elizabeth to the Custodian of St Mary's Hall now hangs on the wall of this room.

The Hall is in excellent condition. It was built between 1340 and 1342 for the merchant guild of St Mary and enlarged between 1394 and 1414 for the united Trinity Guild. It was extensively altered at the end of the 15th century. The principal room is the magnificent Great Hall on the first floor which has a late 14th-century timber roof and a tapestry from around 1500. Below the Great Hall is a large vaulted undercroft. Caesar's Tower is a stone structure which may have had its origins as a building within the outer bailey of Coventry Castle.

The Shrewsburys also went to Coventry to assist with the guarding of the royal prisoner as they were back in favour with the English Queen.

News was received from Scotland in January 1570, that the Earl of Moray had been shot and killed in the streets of Linlithgow (B18). The assassin was James Hamilton of Bothwellhaugh who had fought for Queen Mary at the battle of Langside. Moray's body was taken to Edinburgh and interred in the south aisle of the Kirk of St Giles. John Knox preached a sermon to 3,000 mourners. A new Regent would have to be appointed in his place, and Elizabeth finally selected Matthew, Earl of Lennox, father of Henry Stuart, Lord Darnley, and grandfather of the young King. The news must have deeply disturbed Mary on both counts. Whatever she had thought of Moray and the way he had treated her in the past, his death would bring further unrest in Scotland. Elizabeth, aware of the vulnerability of the situation, gave orders for the royal prisoner to be moved back from Coventry to Tutbury since the Northern Uprising had fizzled out. The guard was doubled and the severity of Tutbury was once more upon her. But spring was on its way and with it the possibility of a move to a more pleasant place.

Mary was back under the sole charge of the Shrewsburys. There had been no repercussions in England from Moray's murder so Elizabeth granted permission for a move to another of the Shrewsbury houses at Chatsworth (F7).

The present house at Chatsworth, the home of the Duke and Duchess of Devonshire, was actually built between 1687 and 1707. It was erected on the site of the Elizabethan Chatsworth completed by Bess and set in beautiful parkland alongside the

Notre Dame Cathedral, Paris
Mary was married to the Dauphin of France, Francis, in a lavish ceremony at
Notre Dame on 24 April 1558.

Statue of John Knox, Edinburgh
Mary's most bitter enemy. His statue stands within
the Quadrangle of the Church of Scotland General
Assembly Hall, off Mound Place.

Hermitage Castle
Many rode to Hermitage Castle from Jedburgh to see the wounded
Bothwell on 16 October 1566.

Borthwick Castle
Mary escaped from the Confederate Lords at Borthwick,
disguised as a page boy.

Church of the Holy Rude, Stirling
Mary's son, James, was crowned King at the Church of the Holy Rude in
Stirling on 29 July 1567.

Site of Fotheringhay Castle
Only a mound remains of the once great fortress where Mary was executed
on 8 February 1587.

Tomb of Mary Queen of Scots
Mary's tomb in Westminster Abbey, erected by order of her son,
James VI of Scotland and James I of England. Her body had lain in Peterborough
Cathedral for 25 years before being removed to Westminster.

River Derwent in Derbyshire. The original house occupied exactly the same area as the rectangular part of the existing buildings. The present house contains the Queen of Scots and Leicester Apartments which, according to tradition, occupy the same site as those where Mary stayed during her sojourn.

In earlier times, the nearby village of Edensor stood on a slope overlooking the mansion and stretched over the brow of the hill almost to the site of the present village of the same name. This meant that most of the houses in the village were visible from the hall which then faced eastwards, with its back to the village. Between the house and the river was a walled garden, much of it covered by seven ponds which were designed as an overflow when the river was in full force.

Very little of the Elizabethan era now remains except for the Hunting Tower, set high on a wooded hillside overlooking the house, and the curious moated building just to the left of the main drive beyond the magnificent bridge over the river. This is known as Queen Mary's Bower and is reputedly where Mary used to sit and while away the hours with her ladies, perhaps working at their embroideries. For Mary was an expert needlewoman and was often joined by Bess who was also an enthusiastic embroiderer. The Bower is a raised walled garden reached by a flight of steps.

Such a pleasant place to be in springtime, it is not surprising that it brought a resurgence of life to Mary Stuart. She would have enjoyed hunting, hawking and riding in the vast park. Life seemed much improved though she still harboured a secret desire that a marriage to the Duke of Norfolk might free her from captivity. However, Elizabeth had only offered to release him from the Tower on condition that he renounce all thoughts of marriage with the Queen of Scots. To this he agreed and was released. An offer came from Elizabeth to Mary. She would try and restore her to the throne of Scotland on condition that her son, James, was exchanged as a hostage in England. The Queen of Scots declined.

It was not long before new intrigue became rife and another escape plot was being planned which was also doomed to failure.

It was mainly the idea of some local squires and landowners. They felt that the wild and secluded moorlands around Chatsworth would be ideal for an escape and the idea was to rescue Mary whilst she was out hunting. She would then be escorted across country on horseback to the port of Harwich where a boat would be waiting to take her to the Continent. When first presented with the suggestion, Mary felt the arrangements were shallow and unimpressive. Details were leaked to the Earl of Shrewsbury by George Rolleston, one of the conspirators, and they were soon rounded up and arrested.

While Mary was at Chatsworth she lost one of her closest friends, John Beaton, Master of her Household, who died and was buried in the nearby church at Edensor. The Queen was grieved at the loss of Beaton, who was one of the staunchest and most loyal of her servants. A brass plate to his memory has been retained and can be seen on an inside wall of the present parish church at Edensor. Graves of past members of the Devonshire family can also be seen at the top end of the churchyard including that of Kathleen Kennedy, sister of the late President John F Kennedy. Kathleen was married to Lord Hartington, heir to the Duke of Devonshire, who was killed in an air crash during the Second World War.

After the Chatsworth conspiracy, Mary's place of confinement was once again considered unsafe. William Cecil suggested to Elizabeth the immediate removal of their prisoner to Shrewsbury's most secure house at Sheffield. Arrangements for another journey were therefore put in hand.

It may have been a misty day on 28 November 1570 as Lord Shrewsbury escorted Mary Queen of Scots and her retinue, with a strong force of guardsmen, through the gates of Chatsworth. They would have threaded their way up onto Baslow Edge and along the escarpment of millstone grit of Curbar and Froggatt Edges and on through the fine estate of Longshaw. On top of the windswept heather-clad moorlands, the air would have been fresh as the party descended from Totley Moor into the valley of the River Sheaf. Afterwards, the journey was more gentle as they followed the course of the river. They would have passed the little forges where knives, scythes and other hand tools were manufactured. Approaching the little town of Sheffield with its forbidding castle and elegant parish church, they might have noticed its fine setting surrounded by seven hills. As the entourage reached the fortress, the drawbridge was lowered and they crossed into the confines of Sheffield Castle (F1). Little did Mary know that this was to be her main prison for almost another fourteen years, longer than the total time she had lived in Scotland. The years of desolation were now upon her.

CHAPTER 13

The Ridolfi Plot

SHEFFIELD CASTLE WAS BUILT in the 12th century by William de Lovetôt at the confluence of the Rivers Don and Sheaf, providing a natural moat on two sides. The original Saxon hamlet – Escafeld – had first been established there. The castle and manor of Sheffield (F1) then passed to the de Furnival family and remained with them for two hundred years during which time it was burnt down in 1265. Five years later, work started on the re-building of the castle. In 1383 the Talbot family inherited the manor by marriage, and in 1442 John Talbot was created 1st Earl of Shrewsbury. Over the years improvements and extensions had been made to the buildings so that it had become a formidable fortress and the strongest property on the Shrewsbury estates. Only a few frag-

Sheffield Manor Turret House

ments of wall of the original Sheffield Castle (F1) remain, preserved in a room behind the Castle Market.

As one of the additions to the estate, a hunting lodge was established high on a hill in the centre of Sheffield Park about a mile from the castle. The 4th Earl enhanced the building, known as Sheffield Manor (F2), and it was here that Cardinal Wolsey stayed just prior to his death, before he could stand trial for high treason. It was ironic that Mary Queen of Scots, another figure who had fallen from greatness, should pace the same corridors four decades later. Ruins of the Wolsey Tower and Long Gallery still stand, as well as excavated foundations of twin brick-faced towers and the southern half of one of the wings.

The perfectly preserved Turret House – the only roofed building on the site – still retains its original features. The second floor contains two rooms which are known as Queen Mary's Rooms. One has splendid heraldic motifs of the Shrewsbury family over the fireplace. The ceiling is of fine plasterwork containing a number of embellishments such as thistles, crowns and royal arms. The patterning on the wall frieze is identical to the design on some of Mary Stuart's needlework which lends credence to the possibility that she would have used the building in some way – perhaps as a summer house where she could take refreshment, watch the hunt across Sheffield Park, or spend a few quiet hours at her embroidery. In 1873 the building underwent a faithful restoration under the supervision of the 15th Duke of Norfolk, a successor to the Earls of Shrewsbury to Sheffield Manor.

Although Mary's main prison was Sheffield Castle, she was allowed occasional visits to the Manor, especially while her rooms were being 'sweetened' or cleaned. In addition, she had several short breaks away – seven to Chatsworth, five to Buxton and two to Worksop Manor, since destroyed by fire and replaced. In total, the time she was actually allowed to leave Sheffield during her fourteen years there amounted to twelve weeks and two days.

The Queen of Scots had not been in Sheffield long before a much wider conspiracy began to unfold. In August 1570 the Duke of Norfolk was released from the Tower of London and began to be involved in a new plot inspired by an Italian banker named Roberto Ridolfi.

Ridolfi was a Roman Catholic who had first come to England after the marriage of Queen Mary Tudor and Philip II of Spain. He was brilliant at financial matters and soon became an advisor to many influential noblemen at the English court. In his dealings at court, Ridolfi's relationships began to drag him into the political arena. Not unnaturally, his sympathies inclined towards his own religion. Elizabeth and her ministers were impressed by the Italian's capabilities. This confidence in him proved useful. Soon Ridolfi began consulting with Mary's envoy, the Bishop of Ross, regarding the hatching of a new plot for her freedom.

The idea behind the scheme was to encourage an invasion of England from the Netherlands, led by the Spanish General, the Duke of Alva. This would be supported by a Catholic uprising within England. The planned outcome was that Mary would be freed and Elizabeth taken prisoner. The Queen of Scots would then be placed on the throne of England with the Duke of Norfolk at her side as Consort.

Meanwhile, William Cecil, who had been given the title Lord Burghley by Elizabeth, paid Mary a visit in Sheffield, the object of his mission being to place before her documents which would lead to an alliance between her and Elizabeth. Once again, the conditions were the same as had been put to Mary on a previous occasion. She must give up all claim to the English throne, agree not to proceed with any marriage settlement without the initial approval of Elizabeth, and, should she be restored to the throne of Scotland with English assistance, send her son, James, to England as hostage. These proposals did not get very far.

By March 1571, plans had been drawn up regarding the Ridolfi Plot, and the Duke of Norfolk had to sign a statement proclaiming his religion. He agreed to lead an army provided by Philip II of Spain to remove Elizabeth from the English throne.

Ridolfi travelled to Brussels for a meeting with the Duke of Alva.

A man named Charles Baillie was enlisted, another keen supporter of Mary Stuart, a Catholic, and he acted as messenger to carry letters back to England for the Bishop of Ross and for Norfolk.

Information about the Ridolfi Plot filtered back to the English court and reached the ears of Walsingham, Elizabeth's master spy-catcher. A trap was set for Baillie. He was seized at Dover and the letters he was carrying were confiscated. In order to obtain a confession from him, he was subjected to excruciating torture.

All this implicated the Queen of Scots and Norfolk. When it was discovered that he had been forwarding money to Mary's supporters in Scotland, Norfolk was re-arrested and taken back to the Tower of London. The Bishop of Ross was also taken prisoner. Under threat of torture, he confessed not only to his involvement in plans for the English invasion by foreign armies but also to the fact that money was being provided by papal authorities in Rome to fund the scheme. The Bishop's confession proved most injurious to Mary, for it was not only inaccurate but slandered her to the point of defamation.

In January 1572 Norfolk was tried for high treason and condemned to death. He was executed the following June. Ridolfi remained abroad and escaped a fearful fate in England.

Whatever Mary's true feelings for Norfolk, she bitterly mourned his death. It would have been her one chance not only of freedom but also to resume married life again after all the indignities she had suffered over the previous two years. She was confronted with accusations that she had been involved in the Ridolfi affair but strongly denied these. The only admission Mary would make was that she had written letters to the Kings of France and Spain respectively and also the Pope, seeking help towards the restoration of her throne in Scotland.

All the plots which had been hatched to release Mary were fated by two weaknesses. One was an over-optimistic assessment of the willingness of Roman Catholics in England to turn against Queen Elizabeth. The other was the reliance on foreign support which would not have been forthcoming without there first having been a rebellion in England. None of the attempts ever got off the ground. The Northern Uprising was a good example of this.

After the Ridolfi plot, Elizabeth's ministers urged her to put Mary Stuart on trial for her supposed part in the schemes. Elizabeth felt that a queen should not be subject to trial by lesser mortals. All she did was allow a Bill to be passed to the effect that Mary be deprived of her claim to the English throne and would be brought to trial should she be discovered plotting again in the future.

1572 proved to be a fatal time for the Roman Catholic Church in England as there was a sudden upsurge against it, brought about by an incident in France which was one of the most blood-curdling of all time. It took place in Paris on 24 August – the Eve of Saint Bartholomew. A signal was given for Catholics in the French capital to attack the Protestant Huguenots. Many atrocities were committed, and the terror gained ground as it spread through the rest of France. In Paris alone, nearly 4,000 Huguenots were butchered. In Rome, the Pope ordered a medal to be struck to commemorate the occasion. The massacre was led by Mary's cousin, Henry, 3rd Duke of Guise, who was leader of the Catholic League in the French Wars of Religion. The affair turned most of Protestant England against the Catholics, and Protestants everywhere united in their call that Catholicism was never to be re-established. This brought about a wave of unpopularity against Mary Stuart.

The Duke of Guise eventually lost favour with the French King, Henry III, who resented his popularity with the Roman Catholics and the Parisians who had rejected the monarchy. In 1588 Henry called his Estates General to Blois, determined to deal with Guise. Whilst Guise was dining in the château at Blois (D8), he was handed a napkin concealing a note of warning – 'Take care. Someone is about to harm you.' Guise read the note and wrote on it 'No one would dare', then threw it under the table. The next day he was grabbed by some of the King's men and stabbed to death. Just over three months later, Henry III was assassinated.

Due to the unpopularity of the Catholic faith in England, Elizabeth began to feel a little more secure on her throne, and she made an act of leniency toward Mary. Since the Queen of Scots had been kept in captivity, her health had gradually deteriorated. After constant pleas to Elizabeth, permission was finally given for the occasional visit to Chatsworth, Worksop Manor and Buxton. At Buxton, the highest town in England, Mary was allowed to take the spa waters – first discovered by the Romans – in an effort to bring about some relief for her recurring rheumatism caused by having spent so much time in cold, draughty castles and houses.

In Buxton, Mary lodged at the Old Hall (F8), a building which once stood on the site of the present Old Hall Hotel which incorporates features and sections of the original house. The building dates back to 1573 and was erected by the Earl and Countess of Shrewsbury with the permission of Queen Elizabeth to provide accommodation for Mary Stuart during her occasional visits. Many prominent people stayed at the Hall including the Earls of Leicester, Pembroke and Suffolk and Lord Burghley. At one stage, it was a regular meeting place for the highest in the land and became known as the house of royal intrigue. Some said that the future of England was determined more in the hall in Buxton than at the English court in London. Mary reputedly scratched her message of farewell to Buxton with a diamond ring on one of the bedroom panes. 'Buxton, whose warm waters have made thy name famous, perchance I shall visit thee no more. Farewell.'

When the 3rd Earl of Devonshire rebuilt the hall in 1670, he incorporated some of the original building behind the existing facade and extensions. The 5th Duke of Devonshire built the Royal Crescent and Pump Room in 1784 and popularised Buxton as a spa town. In the 18th century, a large stone bath, thought to be Roman, was discovered next to the Old Hall. Spa water can be sampled in Buxton to the present day.

During one of her five visits to Buxton, Mary met the Earl of Leicester who had gone there to find some ease from gout. Whether his visit was coincidental or not is questionable. The popular theory was that Elizabeth sent him to spy on the Queen of Scots. Mary would undoubtedly have discussed her living conditions and predicament with Leicester in an effort to persuade him to use his influence with the English Queen to try and improve her lot.

Tradition has it that Mary Queen of Scots paid a visit to nearby Poole's Cavern, a cave set into a hillside above the spa town. Visitors are shown a stone pillar named after Mary, supposedly showing how far the Queen of Scots walked into the cavern to see the stalactites and stalagmites. Whether or not somebody with advanced rheumatism and arthritis in their bones would venture into such a damp atmosphere is debatable. Whatever the truth, it adds a romantic flavour to any visit there.

In August 1574, Mary suffered another blow with the death of her devoted Secretary, Pierre Rollett. He was interred in Sheffield Parish Church, now the Anglican Cathedral. In the Chapter House is a beautiful stained-glass roundel depicting Mary with Rollett, her Secretary. The entry of his burial can be inspected in the parish registers. He was replaced by Claude Nau, who was chosen by the Duke of Guise and the Cardinal of Lorraine.

Relations between the Earl of Shrewsbury and his Countess were going from bad to worse. Bess had always been a schemer as the evidence from her four marriages proves, furthering her own well-being and marrying two of her own children into the Talbot family. Yet, despite her marital differences with Shrewsbury and the difficult circumstances surrounding their holding of the Queen of Scots, they had to be seen to be working in harmony. Bess also had to maintain a certain relationship with Mary and, over the years, their friendship wavered back and forth. When the Queen of Scots was feeling particularly vulnerable and low in spirits whilst in mourning for the Duke of Norfolk, she turned to Bess for friendship and consolation. The Countess could not but feel a certain amount of sympathy towards her. Unknown to the Earl, Bess offered to act as mediator between Mary and the Countess of Lennox, her mother-in-law by her marriage to Darnley. Lady

Lennox had never forgiven Mary Stuart for her supposed part in the murder of her elder son.

Margaret Douglas, Countess of Lennox, had a younger son, Charles Stewart, who, like his elder brother, had the blood of both royal houses of Tudor and Stewart in his veins. Bess knew that one day Charles Stewart might also have a strong claim on the English throne. Word had been received that Lady Lennox and her son, Charles, were journeying to London from the North of England. Bess offered to meet the Countess on Mary's behalf and invited her and her son to Rufford Abbey (F4) in Nottinghamshire, another of the Shrewsbury houses. Bess suggested that Rufford would be a good place for them to break their journey for a couple of days before resuming their travels to London.

Rufford Abbey displays examples of every kind of English architectural style from the 12th to the 19th centuries, both ecclesiastical and secular. In 1148, the Earl of Lincoln founded an abbey at Rufford for Cistercians as an annexe of Rievaulx Abbey in Yorkshire. Monks occupied the site until 1536 when the Abbey and estates passed to secular ownership. In the following year, it was acquired by the 6th Earl of Shrewsbury. The Abbey became derelict and a grand country house was built by Shrewsbury. Today, only parts of the Abbey and house remain, mainly in ruins, though sections have been restored. It is surrounded by a beautifully maintained country park and great lake and is part of the region known as Sherwood Forest and The Dukeries.

Very conveniently -- perhaps deliberately – Bess took another of her unmarried daughters, Elizabeth Cavendish, to the meeting with Lady Lennox and her son. Bess must have been highly delighted when the young Elizabeth and Charles fell hopelessly in love. She was not long in persuading Lady Lennox to agree to an early wedding between the young couple in the private chapel at Rufford. Fortunately for Bess, the Countess had fallen ill on her travels and this extended their stay at Rufford, giving Bess the necessary time to make the wedding arrangements before anyone could object. No doubt she was bedazzled and excited by the thought that, one day, one of her daughters might become Queen Consort of England. And if she had a child? The thought would have raced through her mind that she herself might possibly become grandmother to a future English monarch.

All court betrothals had first to seek the sanction of the Sovereign and this had not been done. It was not until after Elizabeth Cavendish and Charles Stewart were married that Queen Elizabeth was informed. She was furious and issued warrants for the arrest of Bess and Lady Lennox. They were both committed to the Tower of London. The Earl of Shrewsbury, when he discovered what had taken place without his knowledge, found it hard to forgive his wife. Bess was distressed by her husband's attitude. However, after three months of imprisonment, Bess was released and received news that her daughter, Elizabeth, was pregnant. This had been her greatest hope and she knew that she was now within striking distance of her goal. The baby was a girl and christened Arabella Stewart, and she was in direct line of succession to the English throne. Bess saw that she must take the child in hand and school her in court etiquette, to achieve her most cherished ambition – to secure the throne for her granddaughter. Through Arabella, she could wield power at court. The Queen of Scots also found a new interest in the baby Arabella and devoted much time to looking after the child. This continued for some months until the rift between the Shrewsburys widened. Bess began to intimidate the Earl with accusations that he was over-friendly with his royal ward.

Arabella's father, Charles Stewart, died after two years of marriage. This left his young daughter only one step away from the throne. Bess took her daughter, Elizabeth, and her granddaughter into her own household. She set out to try to persuade the English Queen to name Arabella Stuart as her heir. Bess felt she had a good chance as the child had been born in England. But Queen Elizabeth was not to be drawn one inch.

Other forces were also at work and suggestions were being made to Elizabeth that King James VI, Mary's son, should be named as heir. He would then become King of both Scotland and England and unite the two countries under one ruler.

The strain on the Shrewsbury marriage had now almost reached breaking point and this was due, in the main, to the strain of holding Mary. In an attempt to hasten the departure of the Queen of Scots from their household, Bess began to spread rumours of an affair between Shrewsbury and his prisoner. She wrote to Elizabeth accusing Mary and the Earl of adultery. Mary Queen of Scots retaliated by drafting a letter to her royal cousin in which she described Bess as always mocking the English Queen and making fun of her appearance. Shrewsbury and Bess were summoned for separate audiences with Elizabeth.

In her wisdom, Elizabeth must have understood the situation and realised the strain under which they had both been placed for so many years. The Earl was duly admonished whilst Bess was told to curtail her wagging tongue in future. The Queen of Scots wrote again to Elizabeth completely refuting any affair between herself and the Earl. Elizabeth may have seen that this was a quarrel between two malicious women, the Earl having become a pawn between them.

It is interesting to consider the influence and effect the holding of Mary Stuart had on the Shrewsbury household. Initially, the upkeep of such a high-ranking political state prisoner and the necessary security would have proved a costly business. Shrewsbury constantly pleaded with Elizabeth for more funds. The response was always negative, with perhaps a suggestion that Mary's retinue might be reduced. This was done on several occasions to the protestations of the Queen of Scots. Perhaps she could contribute something toward her own upkeep? After all, it was well known that she frequently received dowries from the courts of France and Scotland. These, she always maintained, had all been spent. Mary Stuart bombarded Elizabeth with letters regarding the continual reduction in her standard of living. The letters fell on deaf ears and the English Queen maintained that Shrewsbury was entirely responsible for her well-being and security. After all, such an important prisoner who could threaten the security of England had to be well guarded. Costs for this increased as each plot or counter-plot was uncovered. The Earl knew full well he dare not risk letting his ward escape or he would be in serious trouble. The very tight security measures meant that every member of the Shrewsbury family was also subject to rigorous controls. They each had to be vetted before being allowed to enter or leave any establishment where Mary was incarcerated. There were no exceptions to the rule and every time a relative came to visit the Earl and Countess, they had to comply with the same regulations as anyone else. This lack of freedom of movement annoyed Bess.

From Shrewsbury's point of view, he had been placed in an impossible situation, being harried by three demanding women. It is not surprising that he weakened and began to seek out more gentle female companionship. This was provided by one of the servants in his own household, a girl named Eleanor Britton.

The rift between the Shrewsburys never healed. The years of frustration which Shrewsbury had had to endure had left him completely worn out, both physically and mentally. Finally, after much pleading by the Earl, Elizabeth agreed that his ward would be transferred to another gaoler. As a reward for his loyalty and efforts, Shrewsbury was created Earl Marshal of England.

The years of captivity had taken a great toll on Mary. Her hair had begun to turn grey so she resorted to using hairpieces and wigs. The pain in her side had grown much worse and arthritis had attacked her bones. Any journey she undertook would have proved uncomfortable. It was not until 1582 that Mary was allowed to ride in a coach at Sheffield and Chatsworth.

In 1583 a further plot had been uncovered in which Francis Throckmorton, a Catholic, and a relative of Queen Elizabeth's former ambassador, Sir Nicholas Throckmorton, had been discovered carrying letters from Mary agreeing to a Spanish invasion of England and the release of Mary Queen of Scots. Prior to his execution, Throckmorton made a full confession which implicated Mary, stating that she was aware of every part of the plan. In

August 1584, Mary was placed in the custody of Sir Ralph Sadler, who escorted her to Wingfield (F6). A long sigh of relief must have been heard in the Shrewsbury household as the royal captive's entourage finally crossed the drawbridge of Sheffield Castle after so many years of restriction, suspicion and uncertainty. Once they had been relieved of their responsibility as custodians, the Shrewsburys ceased the charade of married life and went their separate ways. Bess always maintained that, despite what had happened, she still held some affection for her husband. The feeling was not reciprocated by the Earl who went to live with his mistress at a house in Handsworth, then a small village to the east of Sheffield. She used him to her advantage and stole many of his assets. Shrewsbury died at Sheffield Manor, almost a broken man, in 1590.

Meanwhile Bess moved to Hardwick Hall (F3) and continued with her rebuilding project and the schooling of Arabella. When she was informed of the Earl's death, she set about arranging a lavish funeral for him. Before he died, an elaborate tomb had been erected in the Shrewsbury Chapel at Sheffield Parish Church (F1). All the townsfolk of Sheffield turned out for the occasion of his burial and much homage was paid to the former Lord of the Manor.

Despite their earlier estrangement, the Earl had left Bess a fortune and, with this, Bess was able to finance the building of a new Hardwick Hall (F3) at the side of her former home and birthplace. It was not completed until 1597. To say that she was fanatical about the project is an understatement. She set about working with the architects, advising the stonemasons and, in fact, put herself in sole charge of the whole building operation. Her plan was to create a building so great and fine that its like had never been seen before. Bess wanted a feeling of space and light. Hence, large rooms were an integral part of her design and included a Long Gallery and High Great Chamber, both suitable for state occasions. Her design also included great expanses of windows which soon gave rise to the saying, 'Hardwick Hall – more glass than wall'.

Today, Hardwick Hall remains as a monument to the ingenuity and skills of the Countess of Shrewsbury as a housebuilder, a constant reminder of her mastery and one of the finest examples of late Elizabethan architecture in Britain. The initials ES for Elizabeth Shrewsbury are significant at the top of each of the hall's six towers, proclaiming to the world her illustrious achievement. The house remained one of the Duke of Devonshire's family homes but, due to crippling death duties, it was handed over to The National Trust in 1956. It remains much as Bess left it when she died. Though Hardwick was never visited by Mary Queen of Scots, there is much of her memorabilia to be seen. These include samples of needlework, a room dedicated to the captive Queen, a statue of Mary, and a range of paintings of Queen Mary and her contemporaries during her years as a prisoner. The Long Gallery contains the well-known 'Sheffield' portrait of Mary in captivity.

In the autumn of 1584, further instructions were issued by Queen Elizabeth that Mary Stuart was to be moved from Wingfield for greater security. She was to be transferred to the hated Tutbury Castle (F10) in January 1585, when weather conditions were at their worst. The English Queen was advised by two of her ministers, Lords Burghley and Walsingham, that there would always be threats of Catholic plots whilst the Queen of Scots was alive. They suggested the time had come to bring the situation to a conclusion. It was put forward that the matter should be taken into their own hands. A trap would be set for Queen Mary and her conspirators once and for all. Reluctantly, Elizabeth agreed.

The plan was to move Mary Stuart first to another gaoler, Sir Amyas Paulet, an ardent Puritan. Paulet had been fully briefed by Burghley and Walsingham on what they were hoping to achieve. It would then be a matter of time before Mary was finally brought to justice.

CHAPTER 14

The Babington Plot

ANTHONY BABINGTON HAD FIRST been introduced to Mary Queen of Scots in 1571. In May of that year, Shrewsbury wrote to Lord Burghley about the death of one of his near neighbours at Wingfield, Babington of Dethick, with whom he had been on very friendly terms. The Earl asked if he could have the wardship of Babington's young heir, and the request was granted. It was thus that the young Anthony Babington first entered the Shrewsbury household at Wingfield Manor as a page boy. He was destined to play a key role in Queen Mary's downfall.

The hamlet of Dethick (F5), where he was born, is not far from Matlock in Derbyshire. Part of the original Babington manor remains in the form of a fine 16th-century barn belonging to Church Farm. The Babington family coat of arms can be distinguished on the gable end. Other parts of the Babington manor are incorporated in the barns and buildings of the adjacent Manor Farm. Close by stands the fine 13th-century Church of St John the Baptist which had many associations with the Babingtons. No burials took place in either the church or the churchyard, but were carried out in nearby Ashover. Certain Babingtons were buried there and the parish church contains a tomb with the reclining figures of Thomas Babington and his wife.

The original manor of Dethick is now split into several units. It retains an atmosphere of tranquillity which is only disturbed by the occasional chugging of a tractor and the sounds of farm animals. Dethick is not very

The Babington Plot

147

is not very easy to find and is best approached from the road between the villages of Crich and Cromford. The turning is at Holloway where the building known as Lea Hurst was once the home of Florence Nightingale, the heroine of the Crimean War. The whole area is regularly used for the filming of the television series *Peak Practice*.

Once Anthony had entered the Earl of Shrewsbury's household at Wingfield (F6), he became familiar with the routines surrounding Queen Mary and soon became acquainted with others in her retinue which was made up of French, Scots and English servants, some of who had been recruited locally. The Queen still had her own Master of the Household, secretaries, a surgeon, physician and apothecary, reader and embroiderer, tailors, grooms and ladies of the chamber. These were to dwindle as time went by and Mary's position grew more desperate.

Babington had been brought up as a Roman Catholic and the Queen would have been pleased to have in her company one so young and of the same religion. As he grew to manhood, he became more and more involved with religious factions and, at the age of eighteen, went to London and joined a secret society of Catholics. He went to France in 1580 and became involved with other Catholics who craved a Catholic monarch on the English throne. It was not long before Babington became a messenger between Queen Mary and her Catholic supporters on the Continent. He fell completely under Mary's spell and became passionately devoted to her. The story is told that, disguised as a gypsy, his face and arms stained with walnut juice, he visited her regularly. There is a walnut tree growing in the inner quadrangle outside the ruins of the Queen's rooms at Wingfield. It supposedly sprang from a walnut dropped by Babington on one of his visits.

The youth had a dashing manner and a remarkable ability for organisation. He was soon earmarked by Mary's agents abroad as a potential ringleader for a Catholic uprising in England with a view to overthrowing the English Queen. In 1586, he was selected to play the leading role in a conspiracy which, supported by Spanish arms, was to bring about the assassination of Elizabeth and the release of Mary Stuart. The plan was secretly sent to the Queen of Scots and to Philip II of Spain, who promised to help in what was termed 'this holy enterprise'. Babington himself raised finance by selling off some of his substantial inheritance. However, as happened whenever plots were afoot, most messages to and from Mary fell into the hands of Elizabeth's ministers.

In September 1561, Mary had to part with one of her most loyal servants, the last and closest of the Four Maries, Mary Seton. She had become so ill and infirm that, for her own good, her mistress insisted that she leave. Mary Seton journeyed to France and entered the Convent of St Pierre in Rheims (D21), where Mary's aunt was Abbess.

Whilst Mary was at Tutbury (F10), Lord Walsingham asked Sir Amyas Paulet, the new gaoler, to consider an alternative prison for his ward. It had to have suitable accommodation and security measures for her to be held until the next part of his scheme to trap her was put into operation. Paulet carried out an inspection visit on Dudley Castle (F16), another motte and bailey castle. It is a substantial building with panoramic views from the top of the castle keep as far as the Malvern Hills.

Dudley was of Saxon origin and given by William the Conqueror to Ansculf of Picquigni which was near Amiens in France. By the 16th century the Dudley family had become lords of the manor and were among the most powerful and influential people in the land. The castle had first come into their possession through John Dudley, the Duke of Northumberland, who rebuilt the fortification around 1540. However, he lost favour when he became involved in the plot to put his daughter-in-law, Lady Jane Grey, on the English throne instead of the Catholic Mary Tudor. Along with his son, Guildford Dudley, he was executed for his part in the conspiracy. Another son was Robert Dudley, the Earl of Leicester, once considered as a possible husband for Mary. He was one of Elizabeth's early favourites and the Queen paid a visit to Dudley Castle in 1575. The ownership of the castle later reverted to the de Sutton family.

On completion of the report by Sir Amyas Paulet, it was con-cluded that Dudley Castle was not considered suitable after all. It was surrounded by too many Catholic families and houses which might have become rallying points. His recommendation was that Chartley Manor (F12) in Staffordshire would be more appropri-ate. The property and estate were owned by Sir Robert Devereux, 2nd Earl of Essex. Nearby were the houses of four lieutenants of the shire who were all loyal to Elizabeth – Sir Walter Aston of Tixall Hall, Sir Richard Bagot of Blithfield Hall, Sir Thomas Trentham of Rocester and Sir Thomas Gresley of Colton. All could be relied upon for their support, if required.

A number of letters exist concerning Mary Queen of Scots dur-ing her confinement at Tutbury, Chartley and Fotheringhay which were addressed to Sir Richard Bagot at Blithfield. These were from Sir Ralph Sadler, Sir Amyas Paulet and Robert Devereux, Earl of Essex. Twenty-three of these letters are now in the Staffordshire Record Office in the county town of Stafford and can be inspect-ed on prior application.

Paulet moved Mary from Tutbury Castle in December 1585 to her new prison, Chartley Manor. It was an Elizabethan manor house set in a large park of nearly one thousand acres. There was a castle at Chartley, ruins of which can still be seen standing proudly on a hillside, a well-known local landmark. However, Mary Queen of Scots was not kept in Chartley Castle. Chartley Manor was situated further down the hill, surrounded by a moat and close to a small lake. Only fragments of the original manor survive both inside and around the present-day Chartley Hall which was built during the Victorian era. It is privately owned and not open to the public, nor is access permitted to the castle ruins, which are best viewed from the nearby road affording vistas across Chartley Park, a lush and peaceful place. It is possible to imagine the scene when Mary was occasionally allowed to go riding or hawking as a relief from the boredom of constant confinement.

From the Earls of Chester, the castle and estate passed into the Ferrers family in 1232. William Ferrers was a descendant of

William the Conqueror's standard bearer. On the death of the 6th Baron Ferrers in 1450, Chartley passed to his daughter, Ann, and her husband, Sir Walter Devereux. His great-grandson, Walter, became Elizabeth's favourite, the 1st Earl of Essex, who entertained the English Queen at Chartley in 1575. It was his son, Sir Robert, who had to open up his house to the captive Queen of Scots and her retinue. He was none too pleased when the English Queen forced him to hold Mary Stuart at Chartley Hall. By now, Mary's health had really deteriorated and was beginning to cause concern. Her youth had left her long ago and she had aged prematurely.

The plans being put into action by Lords Burghley and Walsingham for a scheme to incriminate Mary once and for all were well in hand. What Walsingham needed was to provide Elizabeth with sufficient evidence to ensure she would finally agree with them that the Queen of Scots had now become too dangerous to remain alive. They planned to introduce a new member to the household at Chartley. The man's name was Gilbert Gifford. He was a Catholic supporter who had been apprehended by Walsingham and had switched his allegiance to the Protestant side. A secret compact had been made whereby Gifford agreed to act as a double agent. Once Mary and her retinue had settled at Chartley, Gifford was introduced to Mary. There is no doubt that she was swayed by his Catholic background and what appeared to be his genuine support for her cause.

Gifford was also in touch with Anthony Babington and his close friends who were working towards the overthrow of Elizabeth and the release of Mary Stuart. At Gifford's suggestion a scheme was set up to carry messages to and from Mary whilst she was at Chartley. These letters would be carried in a secret compartment of a casket of ale and delivered to Chartley Manor by a brewer from nearby Burton (F14), a town with a long tradition as a centre for the brewing industry. (The Bass Museum is a splendid place to trace the history of brewing in the town.) Messages were sent in code and, unknown to Mary, translated by an expert in coding and forgery. All the coded messages were passed to

Walsingham after they had been translated. By this method, the whole web of intrigue was monitored.

The Babington plot spread through the Low Countries to Spain and the Vatican. Philip II of Spain was to wait for the uprising by English Catholics and the murder of Elizabeth before he would send troops to England. Few Catholics realised that Elizabeth's life was in danger and merely imagined they were supporting the right of Mary Stuart's succession to the English throne. Only Babington and six of his associates were aware of the truth, and, of course, Lord Walsingham.

Once Walsingham was in possession of the full facts, the conspirators were hunted down and arrested. The only evidence now needed to incriminate Mary was her own correspondence and ciphers. News of Babington's arrest was skilfully kept from Mary. He and his co-conspirators were found guilty and on 20 September 1586 were hideously executed on a scaffold erected in St Giles's Fields in London. They were taken down from the gallows before death and their bodies brutally mutilated.

In consultation with Sir Amyas Paulet, a scheme was devised by Walsingham to move Mary and her retinue away from Chartley for a short period so that a full search could be carried out of her rooms in an effort to discover incriminating evidence.

Sir Amyas invited Mary and her ladies to accompany him on a hunt across Chartley Park one morning. Mary, so used to being confined in her chamber, gladly agreed to the suggestion and welcomed the opportunity to ride again, thinking it a kind gesture by her custodian. She had no idea what was about to take place while her back was turned.

The riding party set off in the direction of Tixall (F13), a few kilometres away. Suddenly, from the opposite direction, Mary was confronted by a party of horsemen. She immediately thought that these were her rescuers come to procure her release. She soon discovered that this was not the case. She was challenged instead by Elizabeth's emissary, Sir Thomas Gorges. He spoke of conspiracy against the English Queen by Mary Stuart and declared that she had been guilty of encouraging a Catholic overthrow of the English throne. Instead of being taken back to Chartley with her attendants, Mary was solemnly conducted by a strong force of guards to Tixall Hall with only a physician and one lady to accompany her. Mary's two Secretaries, Claude Nau and Gilbert Curle, were also arrested and taken to London for questioning.

Tixall is quite close to the town of Stafford and nothing remains today of the original Tixall Hall except the splendid Elizabethan Gatehouse built about 1575 for Sir Walter Aston. The Gatehouse has outlasted the two halls to which it gave access, one Tudor, the other Georgian, the latter being demolished in 1927. It is an architectural gem and well worth seeing. A good view of it can be obtained either from the road between the villages of Tixall and Great Haywood, a centre for canal enthusiasts, or from a narrow boat along the nearby Staffordshire and Worcestershire Canal across Tixall Wide. The Gatehouse is owned by the Landmark Trust.

Mary Stuart was kept at Tixall Hall for about a fortnight. In her absence from Chartley, Walsingham's agents moved in and searched her apartments. Correspondence, notebooks, jewels and letters from fellow conspirators were seized. Searches continued and all the incriminating evidence, documents and ciphers were taken to London.

Eventually, the Queen of Scots was taken back to Chartley accompanied by Paulet. As she departed from Tixall, a group of poor villagers gathered before the Gatehouse, clamouring for alms. 'Alas', Mary cried, 'I have nothing to give. For I am a beggar too. All has been taken from me!' At Chartley Mary discovered what had taken place in her absence. Her rooms had been ransacked and all her possessions thoroughly scrutinised or removed. The net around her was closing and all that faced the Queen of Scots were days of gloom, anguish and uncertainty. After her papers had been closely examined, it was decided that Mary Queen of Scots should stand trial under the Act of Association of 1585. A warrant was issued for her arrest. On 21 September, Mary left Chartley on her final journey.

The party made a stop for a few hours of rest at the Manor House, sometimes known as Hall Hill, in the little village of Abbots Bromley (F11) in Staffordshire. According to local belief, Mary left her signature, written with a diamond, on the pane of a latticed window which is now on view in the William Salt Library in Stafford. The journal of her French physician, Bourgoing, states that Queen Mary spent the night at Burton 'and lodged at a local inn'. A short journey on 22 September took them to Ashby-de-la-Zouch Castle (F15) where Mary had stayed previously during the Northern Uprising in 1569. Continuing eastwards, they travelled to Leicester (F19) on 23 September where they stayed overnight at the Angel Inn, near the town wall. A gable end of this building still survives in the Angel Gateway near Gallowtreegate and the Clock Tower in the city centre. There is a wall plaque about Mary Queen of Scots in Leicester's High Street, on the Huntingdon Tower Building which occupies the site of Lord's Place, the Earl of Huntingdon's town house, where Mary also stayed for a night during the Northern Uprising.

The route continued via Withcote Hall near Oakham (F20) where they stayed as guests of Mr Roger Smith, a local gentleman. The present Withcote Hall dates from the 18th century but nearby is a chapel, usually open to visitors, which has a 16th-century exterior. The final stage of the journey took them through the county of Rutland and across the River Welland at Colleyweston where stone slates have been quarried since Roman times. They have graced rooftops in places as far apart as Oxford and Long Island, New York, as well as the castles of Rockingham, Belvoir and Oakham, and the Guildhall in London.

Mary and her entourage headed south across Rockingham Forest to their final destination – Fotheringhay Castle (F21) in Northamptonshire. Thus was completed the Queen's last journey. She knew that the die was all but cast. It was now just a question of time.

CHAPTER 15

Fotheringhay

FOTHERINGHAY CASTLE WAS BUILT at the end of the 11th century. Little now remains of the once mighty fortress except a mound, fosses and a single block of stonework.

Domesday Book records that Fodringeia was one of many enclosures of Rockingham Forest which, in ancient times, covered some 700 square miles. At the time of Edward the Confessor the property was freehold and in 1086 was granted by William the Conqueror to his niece, Judith, wife of Waltheof. His daughter, Maud, married Simon de Liz, who built Fotheringhay Castle about the year 1100. When Simon died, Maud married King David of Scotland, the property passing later to his son Henry and grandsons Malcolm and William who became Kings of Scotland. It passed into other ownerships until falling again to the Crown. Edward III rebuilt the Castle and granted it to his fifth son, Edmund Plantagenet, surnamed de Langley, who founded the powerful house of York. At the end of the 14th century, he initiated the foundation of a College and the building of a Collegiate Church. Richard III was born at Fotheringhay Castle on 2 October 1452, the youngest son of the Duke of York. In the nearby village is the 15th-century Church of St Mary the Virgin and All Saints.

In the year 1586, as Mary Queen of Scots and her escort covered the last few miles of their journey from Chartley, they would have seen Fotheringhay Castle (F21) from some

Mary's Prayer Book and Rosary

distance across the flatlands. The fortress was situated in an elevated position and the gleaming white stone walls and keep would have been clearly visible. It was a typical Norman castle of the motte and bailey type. The castle and gatehouse faced north. The large keep was built on the top of the mound and the inner bailey consisted of a chapel, a great hall and outbuildings. The site was bounded by a moat whilst the River Nene formed part of the southern defence system. Mary was ushered into Fotheringhay and, together with her Ladies, was confined in rooms in the castle keep. The Castle Governor was Sir William Fitzwilliam and he was one of only a few people who showed any kindness towards Queen Mary during her incarceration at Fotheringhay.

On 1 October, the Queen had a visit from her gaoler, Sir Amyas Paulet, who came to inform her that she was to be interrogated by certain Lords. For her own sake, he suggested she confess her guilt. Mary replied that she was conscious of the fact that she had often offended her Maker but, as a Queen and Sovereign, was unaware of any fault for which she should give account to anyone else.

On 8 October commissioners were appointed in London to sit in judgement on Queen Mary. In advance, they were shown letters between the Queen and Babington which had either been decoded or had been seized at Chartley. It was agreed that Mary be brought to trial under the Act of Association which had been passed by Parliament a year earlier, undoubtedly pushed through with the fate of Mary Queen of Scots in mind. It stated that 'twenty-four peers or privy councillors be considered to try any plot or attempt on the life of Elizabeth by any person who purported to claim her crown for their own person'.

Three days after their appointment, members of the commission began to arrive at Fotheringhay. Some were allocated accommodation in the castle and others lodged in the village or neighbouring farmsteads. Amongst those who had been summoned were Burghley and Walsingham and some of Queen Mary's former custodians such as Sir Ralph Sadler, Sir Amyas Paulet and, though completely against his will, Lord Shrewsbury, her longest-serving gaoler. Mary insisted that, because she was still a sovereign, she should not be subject to trial by such a commission. She finally agreed to appear before it in order to defend herself against the single charge against her that she had plotted the murder of the English Queen.

The trial of Mary Queen of Scots began on Wednesday, 15 October 1586 in a room above the Great Chamber of Fotheringhay Castle. Mary entered the room under escort and took her place on a red velvet chair. Opposite, at the other side of the room, was a throne emblazoned with the Arms of England. The throne was for Queen Elizabeth but, of course, she did not attend.

At the opening of the trial, Queen Mary was accused by the Lord Chancellor of having been involved in a plot to murder the English Queen and overthrow her realm. He concluded his statement by explaining that the accused would be given every opportunity to prove her own innocence.

Mary would have nobody represent her and insisted on conducting her own defence. During cross-examination, she maintained she had first entered England as an independent sovereign who came to ask the assistance of her royal cousin, Elizabeth. Therefore, she was not answerable to any court of law but to God alone.

In spite of her constant protestations, the various items of evidence gathered during the Babington plot were produced. Copies of letters, other correspondence, and the translation of ciphers were waved in her face though she was not allowed to examine any item for herself. She also discovered that her two loyal Secretaries, Claude Nau and Gilbert Curle, had been tortured to provide evidence against their royal mistress in advance of the trial. Burghley then accused Queen Mary of having assumed the title of Queen and the Arms of England even when she had been in France. To this, she protested that it had only been done on the insistence of the French King, her father-in-law, Henry II. With dignity, she added that she had never given up her rights to the English throne, nor did she ever intend to do so.

On the second day of the trial, the Queen of Scots was given permission to address the court in person. She went into great detail about the life and sufferings she had had to endure since entering England. She had expected to be treated as any other visiting monarch from a neighbouring country. Describing some of the indignities she had endured, Mary Stuart spoke bitterly of the humiliation she had experienced during eighteen years of captivity. She did, however, admit that she had consorted with other Roman Catholics to try to procure her release. Her intention had been to leave for another country where she would have been allowed to worship openly in the manner to which she was accustomed. Yet Queen Mary implicitly denied she had ever connived with anyone to secure the death of Elizabeth.

The second phase of the trial dealt with the issue of Mary's plans to transfer the crown of Scotland to Philip II of Spain on her death. When questioned about her loyalties should a Spanish army have arrived in England, she said she was not answerable for Spain. She was merely concerned with her own deliverance from captivity and continued support for the Roman Catholic Church.

Despite her brilliant self-defence, it was a foregone conclusion at the end of the three-day trial that the Queen of Scots would be found guilty. She was guilty not only of conspiring against Elizabeth but also to bring about the death of the English Queen and seize the Crown of England for herself. However, the court had no powers to pass sentence on an anointed monarch. The only person who could do that was Queen Elizabeth. The commissioners left Fotheringhay and retired to the Star Chamber in London to pronounce their verdict. Mary Queen of Scots had been found guilty and should be sentenced to death.

Elizabeth hesitated as she weighed up the consequences of allowing a fellow sovereign and such a high profile Roman Catholic to be put to death. On the one hand, Mary remained a constant threat to her own throne, but on the other, she wondered if she might antagonise Catholic countries on the Continent to declare war on England? There was so much at stake. When the Queen of Scots had been at Chartley, it had been suggested that her gaoler, Paulet, might arrange to have her poisoned. That would have settled the matter at one stroke. Not unnaturally, Paulet refused to co-operate and be left with the death of the royal prisoner on his conscience, despite his loyalty to Elizabeth. The fact of the matter was that the Queen of Scots had been condemned by trial and only Elizabeth could authorise a death warrant. The English Queen wrestled with her conscience but could not make up her mind.

Autumn dragged on into winter and Mary became resigned to the fact that her end was drawing near. In the meantime, she could only continue with her needlework and perhaps occasionally listen to a little music that would, by now, be far from joyful. Queen Mary was also plagued by bodily ailments and rheumatism. During this last period of her life she wrote many letters to her friends and supporters including the Pope, the Kings of France and Spain and her cousin, Henry of Guise.

Meanwhile Elizabeth continued to ponder the case. She knew full well that Mary must die but did not want her own hands tainted with her blood. Finally, on 1 February 1587, after great pressure from Lords Burghley and Walsingham and other ministers, she was persuaded to sign the death warrant which would seal the fate of Mary Queen of Scots.

In Scotland, the news of his mother's impending death had been given to James VI. Under the earlier guidance of the Regent Moray and other Lords of the Congregation, he had been schooled in and had adopted the Protestant faith. Not having seen Mary since infancy, he never really knew her, and it was usually damning or distorted accounts which the young King received from others concerning the captive Queen's past and her alleged plotting against the English crown. He therefore showed little sympathy for the plight in which his mother now found herself. Knowing full well that he stood a good chance of inheriting the English throne, James maintained a reasonably amicable relationship with Elizabeth. He was party to an Anglo-Scottish alliance to which he felt committed.

The final act in the story of Mary Stuart's life began seven days later on the morning of 8 February. It is ironic that the previous evening, the person who was given the awful task of announcing to the Queen of Scots that she was to die the following morning was her old acquaintance and gaoler, the Earl of Shrewsbury. As she was given the news, Mary's two ladies, Jane Kennedy and Elizabeth Curle, wept bitterly for their mistress. Queen Mary ate a little supper and composed a letter to her chaplain.

One can imagine the thoughts that must have been running through her mind. Perhaps she reflected on her life in Scotland – her childhood at Stirling Castle, the hasty removal to Inchmahome Priory and the journey to France. Then there were her formative years at the French court where she had grown up and married Francis, the Dauphin, who only reigned as King for seventeen months with Mary beside him as Queen Consort. His death had led to her return to Scotland in 1561 to face religious changes which had taken place during her absence, and her confrontations with John Knox. Perhaps she would have been better staying in France? It was too late now for regrets. Maybe she reflected on her second marriage to the foolish Lord Darnley and the violent murder of her favourite Secretary, David Rizzio. Then there was her disastrous marriage to Bothwell through which she fell from grace and lost the loyalty of her Scottish subjects. There was also her son, King James VI. What would happen to him when she had gone? Why had he never lifted a finger to help her? On hindsight, she would have been better to return to France to take up holy orders at some convent rather than throw herself on the mercy of her English cousin, Elizabeth. Elizabeth – the one person who could now spare her life. She had always pleaded for a meeting with her, woman to woman, but an audience had never been granted.

Mary completed her last letter which was to her brother-in-law, King Henry III of France, at two in the morning. After a little sleep, the Queen of Scots rose at six o'clock and handed gifts to her weeping ladies then went into the chapel to pray alone. It was between the hours of eight and nine when the Queen of Scots received her summons. An entourage had formed including her gaoler, a priest, both of her ladies and other supporters. Her groom took down a crucifix from the chapel wall and, holding it high, led the small procession from the chamber. Mary was dressed in a long flowing black gown over a red petticoat. She wore a white cap on her head and a transparent veil which reached from her shoulders to the bottom of her skirt.

In the Great Hall, the Queen mounted the scaffold which had been erected overnight. There was a crowd of three hundred waiting to witness her execution. There would appear to have been three chairs placed on the scaffold – two were for the Earls of Shrewsbury and Kent, the other, covered with black cloth, with a cushion of black velvet before it, was reserved for the Queen of Scots. On that chair she sat, with absolute composure, while she listened to Beale, the Clerk of the Council, reading the death warrant.

The executioner, Simon Bulle, who had spent the previous night in the house known as Garden Farm in the nearby village of Fotheringhay, then stepped forward. He begged Queen Mary to pardon him for the act he must perform. 'I forgive you with all my heart for now I hope you shall make an end to all my troubles', she responded. She then handed a gold pomander, a rosary and crucifix, and finally her prayer book to her ladies who assisted in the removal of her black overgown. 'Do not weep for me,' she said to them, 'for soon my troubles will be over. I shall at last be free of this cruel world!'

One of the ladies bound her eyes with a gold cloth. Slowly, and with great dignity, the Queen knelt down and placed her head on the block. She then stretched forth her arms and, in Latin, murmured 'Into Your hands, O Lord, I commend my spirit'. The executioner raised his axe. It took three strokes before the head was finally severed.

The executioner took hold of Queen Mary's auburn tresses to hold the head on high and a head with grey hair fell to the ground.

The Dean of Peterborough then cried out to the assembled body of spectators, 'So perish all the Queen's enemies!' Very few of those present answered 'Amen', and it was reported that the Earl of Shrewsbury was openly weeping.

At this point a rather strange thing happened. Mary's little Skye terrier, which had somehow or other followed her into the Great Hall, suddenly crept from under her petticoat. It could not be coaxed away from the head or body of its mistress.

Mary Queen of Scots was only forty-four years of age when she died so courageously. The bells in London rang out and bonfires were lit in the streets for the deliverance of Queen Elizabeth who wept at the blood that had just been shed at her doing. She might well have thought that Mary's death would now put an end to the whole matter, but there would soon be major repercussions. The ghost of the tragic Queen of Scots was to continue to haunt Elizabeth.

Today, gentle breezes waft thistles back and forth on top of the mound where the forbidding fortress of Fotheringhay once stood by the River Nene. My last visit to Fotheringhay was on a chilly January morning after a hard overnight frost had covered the surrounding fields with white. As I walked along the riverside on the opposite bank of the river to the site of the castle, cattle from nearby Castle Farm chewed nonchalantly. The tranquillity of the scene was only disturbed by a flock of mallards zooming overhead. A sudden shiver ran down my spine. I turned quickly and hastened to the wicket gate, to return to the warmth of my car. Icicles were hanging from the four-arched packhorse bridge of grey limestone above the icy swift-flowing waters. I turned to take a last look and saw the tracks I had made across the field of hoar-frost. It was as though the story of Mary Queen of Scots had been frozen in time. I took a handkerchief from my pocket and wiped away a tear.

CHAPTER 16

Requiem for a Queen

NEWS OF THE DEATH OF Mary Queen of Scots spread through England and Scotland – where it was received with mixed feelings – and countries in Europe. In France, it was commemorated with national mourning, and a Requiem Mass was held in Notre Dame Cathedral where Mary had been married to the Dauphin thirty years earlier. She was remembered as both Queen Consort of King Francis II and as Dowager Queen. She had always wished to be buried in France, either at St Denis with other members of the French royal family, or in Rheims where her mother and other Guise relatives were interred. Neither of these wishes was granted.

After her death, the head and body were wrapped in a cloth and, later in the day, her organs were removed and buried secretly within Fotheringhay Castle for fear they would be stolen as relics. Her remains were then placed in a lead coffin and lay in the castle for some months. Finally, arrangements were made for a burial in nearby Peterborough Cathedral (F25). By night, on 30 July, the coffin was taken in procession, with great solemnity, in a coach draped in black velvet, and reached the Bishop's Palace in

Mary's Tomb, Westminster Abbey

Peterborough at two in the morning. On 1 August, a Protestant ceremony was held in the Cathedral, from which Queen Mary's Roman Catholic supporters withdrew. The coffin was then placed in a tomb in the South Presbytery aisle, opposite the tomb of Queen Catherine of Aragon, first wife of Henry VIII, who had been buried in 1536. The sexton who buried both Queens was Robert Scarlett, whose portrait and wall painting may be seen on the west wall of the nave. He claimed to have buried double the actual population of Peterborough.

Peterborough is one of the finest English cathedrals. According to local chronicles, an abbey was first founded on the site in 655 AD by Peada, King of Mercia. It was later sacked by the Danes in 870 AD. The abbey was refounded as a Benedictine house in 960 AD. About ten years later, a second abbey was consecrated by the Archbishops of Canterbury and York in the presence of King Edgar. This was burned down in 1116 and work was started on the present building and took 120 years to complete. For the first 900 years of the existence of a church on the site it was an abbey, until it was consecrated as a cathedral in 1541. Over the years, the building has undergone many changes and additions and has many architectural styles and periods within its fabric. The magnificent West Front was restored between 1896 and 1905. Today there is a plaque on an adjacent pillar to the original site of Mary's tomb, before the removal of her coffin to Westminster Abbey. There is also a small exhibition about her life. A visitor centre is due to open in mid-1999 and will contain other items of Maryana.

After Queen Mary's death, Elizabeth did not sit comfortably on her throne. It was reported by her Secretary of State, Sir William Davison, that she was grief-stricken and hysterical. Davison had replaced Burghley who had been given the office of Lord High Treasurer in 1572.

In 1587, Burghley completed building a magnificent house near Stamford in Lincolnshire, a task which had taken thirty years. Built around a courtyard with towers at each corner, Burghley House (F23) recalls a medieval castle and combines

French, English and Flemish architectural influences. The building contains important letters and documents associated with the Queen of Scots. Burghley is the setting for the annual Burghley Horse Championships.

Lord Burghley died in August 1598 and was buried in the 15th-century St Martin's Church in Stamford (F24), which houses a great monument to this distinguished Elizabethan. His effigy lies on a marble table tomb wearing armour and his Garter robes and insignia. Stamford has been proclaimed 'the finest stone town in England'. The spires and towers of its many ecclesiastical buildings reveal its past importance as a religious centre. It was used as a location for the BBC's adaptation of George Eliot's *Middlemarch*.

Rumours that Philip II of Spain was planning a huge invasion of England had been circulating during 1586. Five months after Mary's death, Sir Francis Drake claimed that he had delayed the planned invasion by the Spanish Armada after a skirmish at Cadiz where he had destroyed thousands of tons of shipping and a large quantity of food and other provisions. This action was dubbed the 'singeing the King of Spain's beard'. Drake then seized Cape St Vincent and blockaded the supply route. However, it was only a matter of time before the Spanish re-organised themselves.

Knowing full well that the death of Mary Stuart had robbed them of any alliance with the English throne, Philip II was determined to claim England by force. He had come to believe that the English crown was his for the taking. He also put forward a claim for himself as the rightful monarch, through his descent from Edward III's son, John of Gaunt, two of whose daughters had married into the royal Houses of Portugal and Castile.

On 3 August 1588 the Spanish Armada sailed into the English Channel where they suffered the most humiliating defeat in Spain's naval history.

As regards the reaction of James VI to his mother's death, some say he showed great sadness and retired to bed without any supper. Other reports state that he remarked gleefully to those about him that, with his mother's death, he was now sole monarch. In

August 1589, aged twenty-three, he married by proxy the fourteen-year-old Princess Anne of Denmark. He met his bride four months later in Oslo. Gradually over the years, he learnt the full facts of his mother's long imprisonment in England and the treatment which had been meted out to her. He must have felt rather guilty at his lack of support for Mary's impossible situation.

Sixteen years after the death of Mary Stuart, Elizabeth died at Richmond Palace on 24 March 1603. Even on her deathbed she had refused to name her heir. Just prior to her final slumber, she nodded approval when she was asked if James VI of Scotland should succeed her? He was then proclaimed King James I of England and thus united the two kingdoms of England and Scotland under one ruler.

Elizabeth was interred in Westminster Abbey (F28) and a lavish tomb with a canopy was prepared by King James for the English Queen. Nine years later, in 1612, after the story of his mother was finally revealed, he arranged for Mary's coffin to be exhumed from Peterborough Cathedral where it had lain for twenty-five years. It was transferred to Westminster Abbey to lie in an even more elaborate tomb than Elizabeth's. The tomb was started in 1607 by Cornelius Cure, Master Mason to the Crown, and completed by his son after his death. The face and effigy of Mary are an idealised youthful portrait. The tomb is situated in the South Aisle, whereas Elizabeth's is in the North Aisle of the Abbey.

Westminster Abbey is one of the most famous and widely visited churches in Christendom. Originally, it was built as part of a Benedictine monastery by King Edward the Confessor. His successor, Henry III, rebuilt the old Norman abbey. The nave was constructed through the Middle Ages. The Henry VII Chapel was erected in the 16th century, and many English monarchs are buried there, the last being George II. The monastery was converted into the Collegiate Church of St Peter in Westminster by Queen Elizabeth during the Reformation.

After William the Conqueror won the Battle of Hastings in

1066, he was crowned in Westminster Abbey on Christmas Day. Nearly every monarch since then, with one or two exceptions (Edward V, Lady Jane Grey, and Edward VIII who abdicated the throne in 1937), have been crowned on Edward I's coronation chair and anointed in the Abbey Church. For hundreds of years, the Stone of Scone was placed just underneath the seat of the coronation chair. It had originally been taken from Scotland by Edward I in 1296 and brought to London. Both the chair and the Stone have been used at coronations ever since. The Stone is now back in Scotland at Edinburgh Castle, having been removed from the Abbey twice on previous occasions. The first time was in 1657 during the period of the Commonwealth when it was used in Westminster Hall at the installation of Oliver Cromwell as Lord Protector. The second was in 1950 when it was returned to Scotland by a group of Scottish nationalists.

Every year, on 8 December, the anniversary of the birth of Mary Queen of Scots, a visit is made to her tomb in Westminster Abbey by members of the Marie Stuart Society. A wreath is placed at the foot of the tomb in remembrance of a Queen who died so bravely.

Popular tradition would have us believe that King James I was responsible for the demolition of Fotheringhay Castle as a result of the reports he received surrounding his mother's untimely death. This was not, in fact, the case, as it had already started to fall into disrepair and neglect shortly after 1587. By 1635 it was reported to be in a ruinous state and was eventually pulled down. Gradually, over the years, local stonemasons and builders either bought or helped themselves to the masonry. Both Wakerley Priory in Rockingham Forest and Fineshade Abbey near Kingscliffe were rebuilt using stones from the site.

Nearby in the town of Oundle stands the Talbot Hotel (F22), formerly known as the Tabret. Stones from the ruins of Fotheringhay Castle were used in 1626 when the Talbot's frontage was rebuilt. In 1638, the oak staircase, which once led to the top room of the castle keep where Mary Queen of Scots was kept, was also installed in the Talbot and remains there to this day. The staircase is divided by a small wicket gate which once marked the boundary of Mary's prison confines. She was never allowed beyond it. It is said that there is the outline of a crown in the wooden balustrade made by a ring on Queen Mary's hand as she gripped the rail on her way to the block. The great horn windows, across which the staircase runs, were also taken from Fotheringhay. These windows, through which Mary watched the preparations for her death, now look out on to the courtyard of the Talbot. A painting by Laslett Pott (1837-1898) is on view in the lounge showing Mary Queen of Scots being led to her execution. There is also a painting in the dining room by C. E. Stewart which depicts Mary sitting in pensive mood as she ponders her uncertain future.

There was a dwelling on the site of the Talbot as far back as 638 AD when a group of monks founded a hostel, serving food, drink and shelter to pilgrims and wayfarers. It was attached to a monastery built by Bishop Wilfrid on the site now occupied by Oundle Schoolhouse. The Talbot is not without its ghost stories. There have been sightings of Mary gazing sadly through the mullioned windows on the stairs, and guests are sometimes awakened by a woman sobbing for many hours during the night. The ghost appears to haunt the stairs and two of the upper bedrooms. Eyewitness accounts have been given of a woman dressed in a long black gown standing at the foot of one of the beds.

Before her death Mary Queen of Scots willed clothing and effects to some of her closest servants and supporters. Items of Marian memorabilia can be seen at different locations. The gold rosary and prayer book she carried on her final journey are on display at Arundel Castle, the ancestral home of the Dukes of Norfolk in West Sussex. The chemise which she wore at the execution can be seen at Coughton Court (F17), a beautiful Elizabethan manor house near Alcester in Warwickshire. It is still owned by the Throckmorton family, descendants of Sir Nicholas Throckmorton, one of the English ambassadors during Queen Mary's reign in Scotland. Another member of the family, Francis, was executed for his part in a plot against Elizabeth. In the musical operetta *Merrie England* by Edward German, Sir Walter Raleigh is banished from court for wooing his future wife, Bessie Throckmorton, in preference to the English Queen.

The chair said to have been that which was provided for the Queen of Scots in which she sat during the reading of the death warrant, was for years kept at All Saints Parish Church, Conington (F26), a small village about thirteen kilometres south of Peterborough. Conington means the King's manor or the 'ton' of the King. For many centuries the property was held by the Royal House of Scotland who were also the Earls of Huntingdon. It may have been through the Earl of Huntingdon, one of Mary's custodians, that the chair was first brought to the church. However, there is another theory. In a book published in 1886, *Fotheringhay and Mary Queen of Scots* by Cuthbert Bede, the chair is described as a large and finely carved abbot's chair which formerly belonged to Peterborough and was seen by Lord Coleraine in Conington Church in 1743. The book states that it may have been sent to Fotheringhay from Peterborough and, on demolition of Fotheringhay, removed to the church at Conington by Sir Robert Bruce Cotton, a cousin of Mary Stuart. The church is early 16th century with later restoration. In June 1999, Queen Mary's chair was removed to Peterborough Cathedral where it is on regular public display.

At Hatfield House in Hertfordshire (F27), built by Lord Burghley's second son, Robert Cecil, later Earl of Salisbury, there is a valuable collection of Mary's letters and a full length portrait of the Queen of Scots during her captivity painted by Oudry. There are also portraits in London at the National Portrait Gallery, and a statue is situated in a niche on the first floor of 143-144 Fleet Street. A signet ring once owned by Mary, and other effects, can be found at the British Museum.

In France, though there are many locations associated with Mary's early years, there are few actual references to her. The reason for this may be that she was not a monarch, but Queen

Consort and later Dowager Queen, and her first husband, Francis, only reigned for a short period. Mary Stuart would not have become involved in state affairs until she grew up, married the Dauphin and became his Consort. The visitor may therefore find it difficult at some locations to discover specific information about Mary's life in France. There are, however, a number of sites with which she was associated where artefacts can be identified; for instance, in Paris there is the Bibliothèque Nationale, the Palais de Justice, the Musée Carnavalet (the best example of a Renaissance mansion on the rue de Sèvignè in the Marais district) which has a small portrait of Mary Stuart in white mourning clothes, and the Jardin du Luxembourg with its statue of Mary. The Musée Conde in Chantilly (D19) – a town synonymous with lace – is also worth a visit, as is Écouen (D18) which houses the National Renaissance Museum.

There are many historic places and museums in Scotland where memorabilia associated with Mary's life can be seen. The 15th-century silver casket given to Queen Mary by her first husband, Francis II, in which the letters said to have been sent by Mary to Bothwell regarding the Darnley murder were discovered, is on show at Lennoxlove, the former Lethington Tower, home of the Duke of Hamilton and Brandon (B8). The Tower was owned for three centuries by the Maitlands, one of whom was Mary's Secretary of State, William Maitland of Lethington, who married Mary Fleming, one of the four Maries. In the Great Hall is a death mask of Mary Queen of Scots and a sapphire ring which was a gift to the family from the Queen. Lennoxlove is a fascinating place, especially beautiful at daffodil time. It is situated on the outskirts of Haddington, and the present Duke of Hamilton, as the senior Duke in Scotland, has responsibility for the upkeep and care of the Palace of Holyroodhouse.

There is a display of Marian momentoes in Edinburgh's new Museum of Scotland (A4). In the section about Mary Queen of Scots, amongst other things there are items from the Penecuik Jewels and a scale model replica of her tomb in Westminster

Abbey. Various portraits of Mary and other members of the Stewart dynasty can be viewed at the Scottish National Portrait Gallery – including an anamorphosis of the Queen of Scots. This is a portrait of Mary's head and shoulders which alternates into an image of a skull. (A10).

A relic which recently came to light was a small football which is now on display at the Smith Art Gallery in Stirling. This was once one of Mary's effects and it was recently re-discovered in a box after its disappearance from the Queen's Room at Stirling Castle in 1570. It is thought that Mary would have officially started a game of football by tossing it from her window to the players below.

Samples of Mary's embroidery can be seen in bed hangings at Scone Palace near Perth, a mansion which has been in the posses- sion of the Mansfield family for nearly four centuries and where the Stone of Scone was situated for almost 500 years.

In England, there are excellent displays of Mary's needlework in bed hangings and other work at Oxburgh Hall, near Kings Lynn in Norfolk. Similar work done by both Queen Mary and Bess, Countess of Shrewsbury, can be inspected at Hardwick Hall (F3) where there are fine portraits in the Long Gallery and a stat- ue of the Queen of Scots at the rear of the house. Hardwick Hall is more or less as Bess left it. A visit was made by Queen Elizabeth II in 1997 to commemorate the 400th anniversary of the comple- tion of the Hall.

But what of Bess herself? She remained at Hardwick Hall for the rest of her life and did all she could to promote the cause of Arabella Stuart, her granddaughter, as the next Sovereign of England after Elizabeth. Arabella was sent to the English court but her behaviour was not to the Queen's liking. She later married William Seymour, Earl of Hertford, in 1610 without the approval of the Sovereign, James I, who imprisoned her in the Tower of London where she eventually died in 1615 at the age of forty.

Bess continued her house-building activities throughout her life and maintained that she would never die whilst she kept on building. During the winter of 1607-8, terrible weather set in which caused the building work on Bess's new house at Oldcoates to be halted. On 13 February 1608, Bess died. She was buried, at her own choosing, in an elaborate tomb which she had prepared for herself in All Saints' Church, Derby, now Derby Cathedral (F9). She did not wish to lie with her fourth husband, Lord Shrewsbury, in his tomb at Sheffield.

In the dynasties which Bess had started through the marriages of her children by her own marriage to William Cavendish, she had set up some of the most illustrious families in Britain. What a character she must have been! The present Duke of Devonshire is descended directly from her favourite son, William. From her daughter, Frances, came the Dukes of Kingston and from them the Earls Manvers. Her eldest daughter, Mary Talbot, became mother-in-law to the Earls of Kent, Pembroke and Arundel, and the present Duke of Norfolk is descended from the latter. From Charles Cavendish who bought Welbeck Abbey from Gilbert Talbot, came the Dukes of Portland. Lady Nina Cecilia Cavendish-Bentinck, cousin to the Duke of Portland and a great-granddaughter of the 3rd Duke who was twice Prime Minister in 1783 and 1807-9, was married to the Earl of Strathmore and Kinghorne. Their youngest daughter, the Lady Elizabeth Bowes-Lyon, married the Duke of York, and they became King George VI and Queen Elizabeth. Through their elder daughter, Queen Elizabeth II, Bess finally achieved her ambition of securing the throne for one of her descendants.

It would also have been a comforting thought for Mary Queen of Scots, although she never ruled England herself, that her line of succession was to extend right down to present day. For every British Sovereign has been her descendant and Queen Elizabeth II is thirteenth in line of descent through the female line from Elizabeth of Bohemia, daughter of King James I of England. Mary's descendants also extend to many other royal houses. Henrietta Anne, the youngest daughter of Mary's grandson, Charles I, married Philippe, Duke of Orléans, brother of Louis XIV

Europe were descended. Mary's influence has been enormous. As she embroidered that cloth of estate with the words, 'In my end is my beginning', how right she was proved to be when one considers the genealogy of her offspring.

Mary was by nature a much kindlier and more gentle person than Elizabeth. The English Queen ruled from her head and always seemed to have the upper hand. Mary was vulnerable, in many ways ill-advised and indecisive, resulting in her becoming a pawn in the hands of nobles and other monarchs. Both Queen Elizabeth and Bess, Countess of Shrewsbury, were strong characters – tough, clever, devious, ambitious and ruthless. As a student of Mary's life and an author, I cannot accept, however, that Mary was entirely innocent of scheming towards the removal of her cousin, Elizabeth. In March 1999 a letter was produced for sale in Germany which is thought to have been kept in government archives in Spain for many years. If it is authentic, it confirms that the Queen of Scots was seeking help from the Kings of France and Spain to re-establish Catholicism in England and backing for her claim to Elizabeth's throne. The 430-year-old coded letter appears to have been written on Mary's behalf from Bolton Castle by one of her secretaries. If it is genuine, it strengthens the case against her.

Few people who have ever lived have attracted as much attention as this Queen. She stands out in Scottish history as the single most romantic and perhaps the most misunderstood of monarchs. Both figuratively and metaphorically, she was head and shoulders above them all! So much has been written about her and there have always been two schools of thought. Her admirers say she was beautiful, fascinating, unfortunate, wronged, and almost martyred. Her critics claim she was wicked, heartless, treacherous, dangerous and, according to the usages of the times when she lived, deserved her awful fate. It is up to the reader, visitor or student of history to decide for themselves. May it always remain so for those who seek to follow her famous footsteps.

Useful Addresses

British Museum,
Great Russell Street,
London WC1B 3DG.
Tel 0171 636 1555

British Tourist Authority,
Thames Tower,
Black's Road,
Hammersmith,
London W6 9EL.
Tel 0181 846 9000

The Churches Conservation Trust,
89 Fleet Street,
London EC4Y 1DH.
Tel 0171 936 2285

Danish Tourist Board,
55 Sloane Street,
London SW1X 9SY.
Tel 0171 259 5959

English Tourist Board,
Thames Tower,
Black's Road,
Hammersmith,
London W6 9EL.
Tel 0181 846 9000

English Heritage,
429 Oxford Street,
London W1R 2HD.
Tel 0171 973 3000

French Government Tourist
Office,
178 Piccadilly,
London W1V 0AL.
Tel 0891 244123

Friends of Sheffield Manor Castle,
Room G44,
Chief Executive's Dept,
Town Hall,
Sheffield S1 2HH.
Tel 0114 273 6923

Great Houses of Scotland,
c/o Scone Palace,
Perth PH2 6BD.
Tel 01738 552300

Historic Scotland,
Longmore House,
Salisbury Place,
Edinburgh EH9 1SH
Tel. 0131 668 8800

Historic Houses Association
(England),
2 Chester Street,
London SW1X 7BB.
Tel 0171 259 5688

Historic Houses Association
(Scotland),
c/o Anderson Strathearn,
48 Castle Street,
Edinburgh EH2 3LX.
Tel 0131 220 2345

The Landmark Trust,
Shottesbrooke,
Maidenhead,
Berkshire SL6 3SW.
Tel 01628 825925

Museums and Galleries
Commission,
Portland House,
Stag Place,
London SW1E 5EZ.
Tel 0171 233 4200

Museum of Scotland,
Chambers Street,
Edinburgh EH1 1JF.
Tel 0131 220 0237

National Gallery of Scotland,
The Mound,
Edinburgh EH2 2EL.
Tel 0131 556 8921

National Library of Scotland,
George VI Bridge,
Edinburgh EH1 1EW.
Tel 0131 226 4531

National Portrait Gallery,
St. Martins Place,
London WC2H 0HE.
Tel 0171 306 0055

The National Trust,
36 Queen Anne's Gate,
London SW1H 9AS.
Tel 0171 447 6700

National Trust for Scotland,
5 Charlotte Square,
Edinburgh EH2 4DU.
Tel 0131 226 5922

Royal Museum of Scotland,
Chambers Street,
Edinburgh EH1 1JF.
Tel 0131 255 7534

Scottish National Portrait Gallery,
1 Queen Street,
Edinburgh EH2 1JD.
Tel 0131 556 8921

Scottish Tourist Board,
23 Ravelston Terrace,
Edinburgh EH4 3EU.
Tel 0131 332 2433

Scottish Tourist Guides
Association,
Old Town Jail,
St John Street
Stirling FK8 1EA.
Tel 01786 447784

Youth Hostels Association,
Trevelyan House,
8 St. Stephen's Hill,
St. Albans,
Hertfordshire AL1 2DY.
Tel 01727 855215

For details of membership of the
Marie Stuart Society, write to:

Marie Stuart Society,
c/o 10 Trysull Gardens,
Merry Hill,
Wolverhampton,
West Midlands WV3 7LD.

Bibliography

BEVERIDGE, James   Linlithgow Palace
(HMSO, Edinburgh, 1983)

BOGDAN, N.Q.   Lochleven Castle
(HMSO, Edinburgh, 1984)

BREEZE, David   A Queen's Progress
(HMSO, Edinburgh, 1987)

CAPPER, Rosi   Mary Queen of Scots' House and Visitor
Centre (Roxburgh District Council, 1989)

CARPENTER, Edward   Westminster Abbey
(Jarrold & Sons Ltd, Norwich, 1971)

CHEETHAM, J. Keith   Mary Queen of Scots – The Captive Years
(J W Northend Ltd, Sheffield, 1982)

COLINSON, Patrick   The English Captivity of Mary Queen of Scots
(University of Sheffield, Department of
History, 1987)

DERRY, John   The Story of Sheffield
(Sir Isaac Pitman & Sons Ltd, London, 1915)

DONALDSON, Gordon   Mary Queen of Scots
(English University Press, 1974)

DONALDSON, Gordon   The Scottish Reformation
(Cambridge University Press, 1960)

DURANT, David N.   Bess of Hardwick
(Weidenfeld & Nicholson, London, 1977)

EDMUNDS, W. HAWKSLEY   Wingfield Manor
(Thomas Brayshaw Ltd, Chesterfield)

EPERON, Arthur & Barbara — The Loire Valley (Christopher Helm Ltd, Bromley, 1989)

FAWCETT, Richard — Edinburgh Castle (HMSO, Edinburgh, 1980)

FAWCETT, Richard — The Palace of Holyroodhouse (Pitkin Pictorials Ltd, Andover, 1992)

FRASER, Lady Antonia — Mary Queen of Scots (Weidenfeld & Nicholson, London, 1969)

FRASER, Lady Antonia — King James (Book Club Associates, London, 1974)

HAMILTON, The Duke of — Mary Queen of Scots – The Crucial Years (Mainstream Publishing, Edinburgh, 1991)

HIGHAM, Rev Canon Jack — Peterborough Cathedral (Pitkin Pictorials Ltd, Lingfield, 1990)

INNES-SMITH, Robert — The Dukeries and Sherwood Forest (English Life Publications Ltd, 1977)

JACKSON, George — The Story of Bolton Castle (Dalesman Books, North Yorkshire, 1976)

LEADER, J.D. — Mary Queen of Scots In Captivity (George Bell & Sons, London, 1880)

LINES, Charles — Hardwick Hall and The Cavendish Story (English Counties Periodicals Ltd, Manchester)

MARSHALL, Rosalind K. — Mary of Guise (William Collins Sons & Co Ltd, London, 1977)

MARSHALL, Rosalind K. — Elizabeth I (HMSO, London, 1991)

MAXWELL-STUART, P.   Traquair House
                      (Jarrold & Sons Ltd, Norwich, 1966)

MONCRIEFFE, Iain   The Royal Palace of Falkland
                      (The National Trust for Scotland, 1983)

MORRISON, N. Bryssom Mary Queen of Scots
                      (The Vanguard Press, New York, 1960)

ODOM, Rev Canon W.   Mary Stuart, Queen of Scots
                      (J W Northend Ltd, Sheffield, 1926)

PARSONS, Harold   Portrait of The Black Country
                      (Robert Hale & Co Ltd, London, 1986)

PLOWDEN, Alison   Mistress of Hardwick
                      (BBC, London, 1972)

RICHARDSON, J.S.   Inchmahome Priory
                      (HMSO, Edinburgh, 1974)

RITCHIE, W.K.   Mary Queen of Scots and the Scottish
                      Reformation
                      (Longman Group Ltd, London, 1979)

ROBERTSON, Ian   France
                      (A & C Black Publishers Ltd, London, 1997)

SIMPSON, W. Douglas   Craigmillar Castle
                      (HMSO, Edinburgh, 1980)

SIMPSON, W. Douglas   Hermitage Castle
                      (HMSO, Edinburgh, 1982)

SOMERVILLE, Robert   Tutbury Castle
                      (Duchy of Lancaster, 1973)

STEEL, David & Judy   Mary Stuart's Scotland
                      (Artus Books, London, 1987)

SWAIN, Margaret — The Needlework of Mary Queen of Scots
(Ruth Bean, Bedford, 1973)

THOMSON, George M. — The Crime of Mary Stuart
(Hutchinson, 1967)

THOROLD, Henry — Staffordshire
(Faber & Faber, London, 1978)

TOMES, John — Scotland
(A. & C. Black Publishers Ltd, London, 1996)

WOODRUFF, Derek — Workington Hall and the Curwens
(Allerdale Borough Council)

WOODWARD, G.W.O. — Mary Queen of Scots
(Pitkin Guides Ltd, Andover, 1971)

Some other books published by **LUATH** PRESS

ON THE TRAIL OF

On the Trail of William Wallace
David R. Ross
ISBN 0 946487 47 2 PBK £7.99

How close to reality was *Braveheart*?

Where was Wallace actually born?

What was the relationship between Wallace and Bruce?

Are there any surviving eye-witness accounts of Wallace?

How does Wallace influence the psyche of today's Scots?

On the Trail of William Wallace offers a refreshing insight into the life and heritage of the great Scots hero whose proud story is at the very heart of what it means to be Scottish. Not concentrating simply on the hard historical facts of Wallace's life, the book also takes into account the real significance of Wallace and his effect on the ordinary Scot through the ages, manifested in the many sites where his memory is marked.

In trying to piece together the jigsaw of the reality of Wallace's life, David Ross weaves a subtle flow of new information with his own observations. His engaging, thoughtful and at times amusing narrative reads with the ease of a historical novel, complete with all the intrigue, treachery and romance required to hold the attention of the casual reader and still entice the more knowledgable historian.

- 74 places to visit in Scotland and the north of England
- One general map and 3 location maps
- Stirling and Falkirk battle plans
- Wallace's route through London
- Chapter on Wallace connections in North America and elsewhere
- Reproductions of rarely seen illustrations

On the Trail of William Wallace will be enjoyed by anyone with an interest in Scotland, from the passing tourist to the most fervent nationalist. It is an encyclopaedia-cum-guide book, literally stuffed with fascinating titbits not usually on offer in the conventional history book.

David Ross is organiser of and historical adviser to the Society of William Wallace.

'Historians seem to think all there is to be known about Wallace has already been uncovered. Mr Ross has proved that Wallace studies are in fact in their infancy.' ELSPETH KING, Director the the Stirling Smith Art Museum & Gallery, who annotated and introduced the recent Luath edition of *Blind Harry's Wallace.*

'Better the pen than the sword!' RANDALL WALLACE, author of *Braveheart,* when asked by David Ross how it felt to be partly responsible for the freedom of a nation following the Devolution Referendum.

On the Trail of Robert the Bruce
David R. Ross
ISBN 0 946487 52 9 PBK £7.99

On the Trail of Robert the Bruce charts the story of Scotland's hero-king from his boyhood, through his days of indecision as Scotland suffered under the English yoke, to his assumption of the crown exactly six months after the death of William Wallace. Here is the astonishing blow by blow account of how, against fearful odds, Bruce led the Scots to win their greatest ever victory. Bannockburn was not the end of the story. The war against English oppression lasted another fourteen years. Bruce lived just long enough to see his dreams of an independent Scotland come to fruition in 1328 with the signing of the Treaty of Edinburgh. The trail takes us to Bruce sites in Scotland, many of the little known and forgotten battle sites in northern England, and as far afield as the Bruce monuments in Andalusia and Jerusalem.

67 places to visit in Scotland and elsewhere.

One general map, 3 location maps and a map of Bruce-connected sites in Ireland.
Bannockburn battle plan.
Drawings and reproductions of rarely seen illustrations.

On the Trail of Robert the Bruce is not all blood and gore. It brings out the love and laughter, pain and passion of one of the great eras of Scottish history. Read it and you will understand why David Ross has never knowingly killed a spider in his life. Once again, he proves himself a master of the popular brand of hands-on history that made *On the Trail of William Wallace* so popular.

'*David R. Ross is a proud patriot and unashamed romantic.*'
SCOTLAND ON SUNDAY

'*Robert the Bruce knew Scotland, knew every class of her people, as no man who ruled her before or since has done. It was he who asked of her a miracle - and she accomplished it.*'
AGNES MUIR MACKENZIE

On the Trail of Robert Service

GW Lockhart
ISBN 0 946487 24 3 PBK £7.99

Robert Service is famed world-wide for his eye-witness verse-pictures of the Klondike goldrush. As a war poet, his work out-sold Owen and Sassoon, and he went on to become the world's first million selling poet. In search of adventure and new experiences, he emigrated from Scotland to Canada in 1890 where he was caught up in the aftermath of the raging gold fever. His vivid dramatic verse bring to life the wild, larger than life characters of the gold rush Yukon, their bar-room brawls, their lust for gold, their trigger-happy gambles with life and love. 'The Shooting of Dan McGrew' is perhaps his most famous poem:

A bunch of the boys were whooping it up in the Malamute saloon;
The kid that handles the music box was hitting a ragtime tune;

Back of the bar in a solo game, sat Dangerous Dan McGrew,
And watching his luck was his light o'love, the lady that's known as Lou.

His storytelling powers have brought Robert Service enduring fame, particularly in North America and Scotland where he is something of a cult figure.

Starting in Scotland, *On the Trail of Robert Service* follows Service as he wanders through British Columbia, Oregon, California, Mexico, Cuba, Tahiti, Russia, Turkey and the Balkans, finally 'settling' in France.

This revised edition includes an expanded selection of illustrations of scenes from the Klondike as well as several photographs from the family of Robert Service on his travels around the world.

Wallace Lockhart, an expert on Scottish traditional folk music and dance, is the author of *Highland Balls & Village Halls* and *Fiddles & Folk*. His relish for a well-told tale in popular vernacular led him to fall in love with the verse of Robert Service and write his biography.

'*A fitting tribute to a remarkable man - a bank clerk who wanted to become a cowboy. It is hard to imagine a bank clerk writing such lines as:*
A bunch of boys were whooping it up...
The income from his writing actually exceeded his bank salary by a factor of five and he resigned to pursue a full time writing career.'
Charles Munn,
THE SCOTTISH BANKER

'*Robert Service claimed he wrote for those who wouldn't be seen dead reading poetry. His was an almost unbelievably mobile life... Lockhart hangs on breathlessly, enthusiastically unearthing clues to the poet's life.*' Ruth Thomas,
SCOTTISH BOOK COLLECTOR

'*This enthralling biography will delight Service lovers in both the Old World and the New.*'
Marilyn Wright,
SCOTS INDEPENDENT

NATURAL SCOTLAND

Wild Scotland: The essential guide to finding the best of natural Scotland

James McCarthy
Photography by Laurie Campbell
ISBN 0 946487 37 5 PBK £7.50

With a foreword by Magnus Magnusson and striking colour photographs by Laurie Campbell, this is the essential up-to-date guide to viewing wildlife in Scotland for the visitor and resident alike. It provides a fascinating overview of the country's plants, animals, bird and marine life against the background of their typical natural settings, as an introduction to the vivid descriptions of the most accessible localities, linked to clear regional maps. A unique feature is the focus on 'green tourism' and sustainable visitor use of the countryside, contributed by Duncan Bryden, manager of the Scottish Tourist Board's Tourism and the Environment Task Force. Important practical information on access and the best times of year for viewing sites makes this an indispensable and user-friendly travelling companion to anyone interested in exploring Scotland's remarkable natural heritage.

James McCarthy is former Deputy Director for Scotland of the Nature Conservancy Council, and now a Board Member of Scottish Natural Heritage and Chairman of the Environmental Youth Work National Development Project Scotland.

'Nothing but Heather!'

Gerry Cambridge
ISBN 0 946487 49 9 PBK £15.00

Enter the world of Scottish nature – bizarre, brutal, often beautiful, always fascinating – as seen through the lens and poems of Gerry Cambridge, one of Scotland's most distinctive contemporary poets.

On film and in words, Cambridge brings

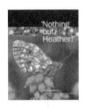

unusual focus to bear on lives as diverse as those of dragonflies, hermit crabs, short-eared owls, and wood anemones. The result is both an instructive look by a naturalist at some of the flora and fauna of Scotland and a poet's aesthetic journey.

This exceptional collection comprises 48 poems matched with 48 captioned photographs. In his introduction Cambridge explores the origins of the project and the approaches to nature taken by other poets, and incorporates a wry account of an unwillingly-sectarian, farm-labouring, bird-obsessed adolescence in rural Ayrshire in the 1970s.

Keats felt that the beauty of a rainbow was somehow tarnished by knowledge of its properties. Yet the natural world is surely made more, not less, marvellous by awareness of its workings. In the poems that accompany these pictures, I have tried to give an inkling of that. May the marriage of verse and image enlarge the reader's appreciation and, perhaps, insight into the chomping, scurrying, quivering, procreating and dying kingdom, however many miles it be beyond the door.
GERRY CAMBRIDGE

'a real poet, with a sense of the music of language and the poetry of life...'
KATHLEEN RAINE

'one of the most promising and original of modern Scottish poets... a master of form and subtlety.'
GEORGE MACKAY BROWN

Scotland Land and People
An Inhabited Solitude

James McCarthy
ISBN 0 946487 57 X PBK £7.99

'Scotland is the country above all others that I have seen, in which a man of imagination may carve out his own pleasures; there are so many inhabited solitudes.'
DOROTHY WORDSWORTH, in her journal of August 1803

An informed and thought-provoking profile of Scotland's unique landscapes and the impact of humans on what we see now and in the future. James McCarthy leads us through the many aspects of the land and the people who inhabit it: natural Scotland; the rocks beneath; land ownership; the use of resources; people and place; conserving Scotland's heritage and much more.

Written in a highly readable style, this concise volume offers an under-standing of the land as a whole. Emphasising the uniqueness of the Scottish environment, the author explores the links between this and other aspects of our culture as a key element in rediscovering a modern sense of the Scottish identity and perception of nationhood.

'This book provides an engaging introduction to the mysteries of Scotland's people and landscapes. Difficult concepts are described in simple terms, providing the interested Scot or tourist with an invaluable overview of the country... It fills an important niche which, to my knowledge, is filled by no other publications.'
BETSY KING, Chief Executive, Scottish Environmental Education Council.

The Highland Geology Trail
John L Roberts
ISBN 0946487 36 7 PBK £4.99

Where can you find the oldest rocks in Europe?
Where can you see ancient hills around 800 million years old?
How do you tell whether a valley was carved out by a glacier, not a river?
What are the Fucoid Beds?
Where do you find rocks folded like putty?
How did great masses of rock pile up like snow in front of a snow-plough?
When did volcanoes spew lava and ash to form Skye, Mull and Rum?

Where can you find fossils on Skye?
'...a lucid introduction to the geological record in general, a jargon-free exposition of the regional background, and a series of descriptions of specific localities of geological interest on a 'trail' around the highlands.
Having checked out the local references on the ground, I can vouch for their accuracy and look forward to investigating farther afield, informed by this guide.
Great care has been taken to explain specific terms as they occur and, in so doing, John Roberts has created a resource of great value which is eminently usable by anyone with an interest in the outdoors...the best bargain you are likely to get as a geology book in the foreseeable future.'
Jim Johnston, PRESS AND JOURNAL

Rum: Nature's Island
Magnus Magnusson
ISBN 0 946487 32 4 £7.95 PBK

Rum: Nature's Island is the fascinating story of a Hebridean island from the earliest times through to the Clearances and its period as the sporting playground of a Lancashire industrial magnate, and on to its rebirth as a National Nature Reserve, a model for the active ecological management of Scotland's wild places.

Thoroughly researched and written in a lively accessible style, the book includes comprehensive coverage of the island's geology, animals and plants, and people, with a special chapter on the Edwardian extravaganza of Kinloch Castle. There is practical information for visitors to what was once known as 'the Forbidden Isle'; the book provides details of bothy and other accommodation, walks and nature trails. It closes with a positive vision for the island's future: biologically diverse, economically dynamic and ecologically sustainable.

Rum: Nature's Island is published in co-operation with Scottish Natural Heritage (of which Magnus Magnusson is Chairman) to mark the 40th anniversary of the acquisition of Rum by its predecessor, The Nature Conservancy.

Red Sky at Night

John Barrington

ISBN 0 946487 60 X   £8.99

'I read John Barrington's book with growing delight. This working shepherd writes beautifully about his animals, about the wildlife, trees and flowers which surround him at all times, and he paints an unforgettable picture of his glorious corner of Western Scotland. It is a lovely story of a rather wonderful life'.
JAMES HERRIOT

John Barrington is a shepherd to over 750 Blackface ewes who graze 2,000 acres of some of Britain's most beautiful hills overlooking the deep dark water of Loch Katrine in Perthshire. The yearly round of lambing, dipping, shearing and the sales is marvellously interwoven into the story of the glen, of Rob Roy in whose house John now lives, of curling when the ice is thick enough, and of sheep dog trials in the summer. Whether up to the hills or along the glen, John knows the haunts of the local wildlife: the wily hill fox, the grunting badger, the herds of red deer, and the shrews, voles and insects which scurry underfoot. He sets his seasonal clock by the passage of birds on the loch, and jealously guards over the golden eagle's eyrie in the hills. Paul Armstrong's sensitive illustrations are the perfect accompaniment to the evocative text.

'Mr Barrington is a great pleasure to read. One learns more things about the countryside from this account of one year than from a decade of The Archers'.
THE DAILY TELEGRAPH

'Powerful and evocative... a book which brings vividly to life the landscape, the wildlife, the farm animals and the people who inhabit John's vista. He makes it easy for the reader to fall in love with both his surrounds and his commune with nature'.
THE SCOTTISH FIELD

'An excellent and informative book.... not only an account of a shepherd's year but also the diary of a naturalist. Little escapes Barrington's enquiring eye and, besides the life cycle of a sheep, he also gives those of every bird, beast, insect and plant that crosses his path, mixing their histories with descriptions of the geography, local history and folklore of his surroundings'.
TLS

'The family life at Glengyle is wholesome, appealing and not without a touch of the Good Life. Many will envy Mr Barrington his fastness home as they cruise up Loch Katrine on the tourist steamer'.
THE FIELD

Listen to the Trees

Don MacCaskill

ISBN 0 946487 65 0   £9.99 PBK

Don MacCaskill is one of Scotland's foremost naturalists, conservationists and wildlife photographers. Listen to the Trees is a beautiful and acutely observed account of how his outlook on life began to change as trees, woods, forests and all the wonders that they contain became a focus in his life. It is rich in its portrayal of the life that moves in the Caledonian forest and on the moorlands – lofty twig-stacked heronries, the elusive peregrine falcon and the red, bushy-tailed fox – of the beauty of the trees, and of those who worked in the forests.

'Trees are surely the supreme example of a life-force stronger than our own,' writes Don MacCaskill. 'Some, like the giant redwoods of North America, live for thousands of years. Some, like our own oaks and pines, may live for centuries. All, given the right conditions, will regenerate their species and survive long into the future.'

In the afterword Dr Philip Ratcliffe, former Head of the Forestry Commission's Environment Branch and a leading environment consultant, discusses the future role of Britain's forests – their influence on the natural environment and on the communities that live and work in and around them.

'Listen to the Trees *will inspire all those with an interest in nature. It is a beautiful account, strongly anecdotal and filled with humour.*'

RENNIE MCOWAN

'*This man adores trees. 200 years from now, your descendants will know why.*'

JIM CHILCHRIST, *The Scotsman*

FOLKLORE

The Supernatural Highlands

Francis Thompson

ISBN 0 946487 31 6 PBK £8.99

An authoritative exploration of the otherworld of the Highlander, happenings and beings hitherto thought to be outwith the ordinary forces of nature. A simple introduction to the way of life of rural Highland and Island communities, this new edition weaves a path through second sight, the evil eye, witchcraft, ghosts, fairies and other supernatural beings, offering new sight-lines on areas of belief once dismissed as folklore and superstition.

Scotland: Myth, Legend and Folklore

Stuart McHardy

ISBN: 0 946487 69 3 PBK 7.99

Who were the people who built the megaliths?

Which great warriors sleep beneath the Hollow Hills?

Were the early Scottish saints just pagans in disguise?

Was King Arthur really Scottish?

When was Nessie first sighted?

This is a book about Scotland drawn from hundreds, if not thousands of years of story-telling. From the oral traditions of the Scots, Gaelic and Norse speakers of the past, it presents a new picture of who the Scottish are and where they come from. The stories that McHardy recounts may be hilarious, tragic, heroic, frightening or just plain bizzare, but they all provide an insight into a unique tradition of myth, legend and folklore that has marked both the language and landscape of Scotland.

Tall Tales from an Island

Peter Macnab

ISBN 0 946487 07 3 PBK £8.99

Peter Macnab was born and reared on Mull. He heard many of these tales as a lad, and others he has listened to in later years.

There are humorous tales, grim tales, witty tales, tales of witchcraft, tales of love, tales of heroism, tales of treachery, historical tales and tales of yesteryear.

A popular lecturer, broadcaster and writer, Peter Macnab is the author of a number of books and articles about Mull, the island he knows so intimately and loves so much. As he himself puts it in his introduction to this book 'I am of the unswerving opinion that nowhere else in the world will you find a better way of life, nor a finer people with whom to share it.'

'*All islands, it seems, have a rich store of characters whose stories represent a kind of sub-culture without which island life would be that much poorer. Macnab has succeeded in giving the retelling of the stories a special Mull flavour, so much so that one can visu-*

alise the storytellers sitting on a bench outside the house with a few cronies, puffing on their pipes and listening with nodding approval.' WEST HIGHLAND FREE PRESS

Tales from the North Coast
Alan Temperley
ISBN 0 946487 18 9 PBK £8.99

Seals and shipwrecks, witches and fairies, curses and clearances, fact and fantasy – the authentic tales in this collection come straight from the heart of a small Highland community. Children and adults alike responsd to their timeless appeal. These *Tales of the North Coast* were collected in the early 1970s by Alan Temperley and young people at Farr Secondary School in Sutherland. All the stories were gathered from the area between the Kyle of Tongue and Strath Halladale, in scattered communities wonderfully rich in lore that had been passed on by word of mouth down the generations. This wide-ranging selection provides a satisying balance between intriguing tales of the supernatural and more everyday occurrences. The book also includes chilling eye-witness accounts of the notorious Strathnaver Clearances when tenants were given a few hours to pack up and get out of their homes, which were then burned to the ground.

Underlying the continuity through the generations, this new edition has a foreward by Jim Johnston, the head teacher at Farr, and includes the vigorous linocut images produced by the young people under the guidance of their art teacher, Elliot Rudie. Since the original publication of this book, Alan Temperley has gone on to become a highly regarded writer for children.

The general reader will find this book's spontaneity, its pictures by the children and its fun utterly charming.
SCOTTISH REVIEW

An admirable book which should serve as an encouragement to other districts to gather what remains of their heritage of folk-tales.
SCOTTISH EDUCATION JOURNAL

LUATH GUIDES TO SCOTLAND
These guides are not your traditional where-to-stay and what-to-eat books. They are companions in the rucksack or car seat, providing the discerning traveller with a blend of fiery opinion and moving description. Here you will find *'that curious pastiche of myths and legend and history that the Scots use to describe their heritage... what battle happened in which glen between which clans; where the Picts sacrificed bulls as recently as the 17th century... A lively counterpoint to the more standard, detached guidebook... Intriguing.'*
THE WASHINGTON POST
These are perfect guides for the discerning visitor or resident to keep close by for reading again and again, written by authors who invite you to share their intimate knowledge and love of the areas covered.

Mull and Iona: Highways and Byways
Peter Macnab
ISBN 0 946487 58 8 PBK £4.95

'The Isle of Mull is of Isles the fairest,
Of ocean's gems 'tis the first and rarest.'
So a local poet described it a hundred years ago, and this recently revised guide to Mull and sacred Iona, the most accessible islands of the Inner Hebrides, takes the reader on a delightful tour of these rare ocean gems, travelling with a native whose unparalleled knowledge and deep feeling for the area unlock the byways of the islands in all their natural beauty.
'

South West Scotland
Tom Atkinson
ISBN 0 946487 04 9 PBK £4.95
This descriptive guide to the magical coun-

try of Robert Burns covers Kyle, Carrick, Galloway, Dumfriesshire, Kirkcudbrightshire and Wigtownshire. Hills, unknown moors and unspoiled beaches grace a land steeped in history and legend and portrayed with affection and deep delight.

An essential book for the visitor who yearns to feel at home in this land of peace and grandeur.

The West Highlands: The Lonely Lands

Tom Atkinson

ISBN 0 946487 56 1 PBK £4.95

A guide to Inveraray, Glencoe, Loch Awe, Loch Lomond, Cowal, the Kyles of Bute and all of central Argyll written with insight, sympathy and loving detail. Once Atkinson has taken you there, these lands can never feel lonely. 'I have sought to make the complex simple, the beautiful accessible and the strange familiar,' he writes, and indeed he brings to the land a knowledge and affection only accessible to someone with intimate knowledge of the area.

A must for travellers and natives who want to delve beneath the surface.

'Highly personal and somewhat quirky… steeped in the lore of Scotland.'
THE WASHINGTON POST

The Northern Highlands: The Empty Lands

Tom Atkinson

ISBN 0 946487 55 3 PBK £4.95

The Highlands of Scotland from Ullapool to Bettyhill and Bonar Bridge to John O' Groats are landscapes of myth and legend, 'empty of people, but of nothing else that brings delight to any tired soul,' writes Atkinson. This highly personal guide describes Highland history and landscape

with love, compassion and above all sheer magic.

Essential reading for anyone who has dreamed of the Highlands.

The North West Highlands: Roads to the Isles

Tom Atkinson

ISBN 0 946487 54 5 PBK £4.95

Ardnamurchan, Morvern, Morar, Moidart and the west coast to Ullapool are included in this guide to the Far West and Far North of Scotland. An unspoiled land of mountains, lochs and silver sands is brought to the walker's toe-tips (and to the reader's fingertips) in this stark, serene and evocative account of town, country and legend. For any visitor to this Highland wonderland, Queen Victoria's favourite place on earth.

LUATH WALKING GUIDES

The highly respected and continually updated guides to the Cairngorms.

'Particularly good on local wildlife and how to see it'
THE COUNTRYMAN

Walks in the Cairngorms

Ernest Cross

ISBN 0 946487 09 X PBK £4.95

This selection of walks celebrates the rare birds, animals, plants and geological wonders of a region often believed difficult to penetrate on foot. Nothing is difficult with this guide in your pocket, as Cross gives a choice for every walker, and includes valuable tips on mountain safety and weather advice.

Ideal for walkers of all ages and skiers waiting for snowier skies.

Short Walks in the Cairngorms

Ernest Cross
ISBN 0 946487 23 5 PBK £4.95

 Cross wrote this volume after overhearing a walker remark that there were no short walks for lazy ramblers in the Cairngorm region. Here is the answer: rambles through scenic woods with a welcoming pub at the end, birdwatching hints, glacier holes, or for the fit and ambitious, scrambles up hills to admire vistas of glorious scenery. Wildlife in the Cairngorms is unequalled elsewhere in Britain, and here it is brought to the binoculars of any walker who treads quietly and with respect.

FICTION

The Bannockburn Years

William Scott
ISBN 0 946487 34 0 PBK £7.95

The Great Melnikov

Hugh MacLachlan
ISBN 0 946487 42 1 PBK £7.95

Grave Robbers

Robin Mitchell
ISBN 0 946487 72 3 PBK £7.99

SPORT

Over the Top with the Tartan Army (Active Service 1992-97)

Andrew McArthur
ISBN 0 946487 45 6 PBK £7.99

Ski & Snowboard Scotland

Hilary Parke
ISBN 0 946487 35 9 PBK £6.99

SOCIAL HISTORY

Shale Voices

Alistair Findlay
foreword by Tam Dalyell MP
ISBN 0 946487 63 4 PBK £10.99
ISBN 0 946487 78 2 HBK £17.99

A Word for Scotland

Jack Campbell
with a foreword by Magnus Magnusson
ISBN 0 946487 48 0 PBK £12.99

The Crofting Years

Francis Thompson
ISBN 0 946487 06 5 PBK £6.95

POETRY

Blind Harry's Wallace

William Hamilton of Gilbertfield
Introduced by Elspeth King
ISBN 0 946487 43 X HBK £15.00
ISBN 0 946487 33 2 PBK £8.99

Poems to be read aloud

Collected and with an introduction by Tom Atkinson
ISBN 0 946487 00 6 PBK £5.00

WALK WITH LUATH

Mountain Days & Bothy Nights

Dave Brown and Ian Mitchell
ISBN 0 946487 15 4 PBK £7.50

The Joy of Hillwalking

Ralph Storer
ISBN 0 946487 28 6 PBK £7.50

Scotland's Mountains before the Mountaineers

Ian Mitchell
ISBN 0 946487 39 1 PBK £9.99

BIOGRAPHY

Tobermory Teuchter: A first-hand account of life on Mull in the early years of the 20th century

Peter Macnab
ISBN 0 946487 41 3 PBK £7.99

Bare Feet and Tackety Boots

Archie Cameron
ISBN 0 946487 17 0 PBK £7.95

Come Dungeons Dark

John Taylor Caldwell
ISBN 0 946487 19 7 PBK £6.95

MUSIC AND DANCE

Highland Balls and Village Halls

GW Lockhart
ISBN 0 946487 12 X PBK £6.95

Fiddles & Folk: A celebration of the re-emergence of Scotland's musical heritage

GW Lockhart
ISBN 0 946487 38 3 PBK £7.95

NEW SCOTLAND

Scotland - Land and Power the agenda for land reform

Andy Wightman
in association with
Democratic Left Scotland

foreword by Lesley Riddoch
ISBN 0 946487 70 7 PBK £5.00

Old Scotland New Scotland

Jeff Fallow
ISBN 0 946487 40 5 PBK £6.99

Notes from the North incorporating a Brief History of the Scots and the English

Emma Wood
ISBN 0 946487 46 4 PBK £8.99

COMING SOON...

On the Trail of Robert Burns

John Cairney
ISBN 0 946487 51 0 PBK £7.99

On the Trail of Rob Roy MacGregor

John Barrington
ISBN 0 946487 59 6 PBK £7.99

On the Trail of John Muir

Cherry Good
ISBN 0 946487 62 6 PBK £7.99

On the Trail of Bonnie Prince Charlie

David R. Ross
ISBN 0 946487 68 5 PBK £7.99

On the Trail of Queen Victoria in the Highlands

Ian R. Mitchell
ISBN 0 946487 79 0 PBK £7.99

Luath Press Limited
committed to publishing well written books worth reading

LUATH PRESS takes its name from Robert Burns, whose little collie Luath (*Gael.*, swift or nimble) tripped up Jean Armour at a wedding and gave him the chance to speak to the woman who was to be his wife and the abiding love of his life. Burns called one of *The Twa Dogs* Luath after Cuchullin's hunting dog in *Ossian's Fingal*. Luath Press grew up in the heart of Burns country, and now resides a few steps up the road from Burns' first lodgings in Edinburgh's Royal Mile.

Luath offers you distinctive writing with a hint of unexpected pleasures.

Most UK bookshops either carry our books in stock or can order them for you. To order direct from us, please send a £sterling cheque, postal order, international money order or your credit card details (number, address of cardholder and expiry date) to us at the address below. Please add post and packing as follows: UK – £1.00 per delivery address; overseas surface mail – £2.50 per delivery address; overseas airmail – £3.50 for the first book to each delivery address, plus £1.00 for each additional book by airmail to the same address. If your order is a gift, we will happily enclose your card or message at no extra charge.

Luath Press Limited
543/2 Castlehill
The Royal Mile
Edinburgh EH1 2ND
Telephone: 0131 225 4326 (24 hours)
Fax: 0131 225 4324
email: gavin.macdougall@luath.co.uk
Website: www.luath.co.uk